GET RID OF WORKSH

VOCABULARY

GROW^th

USER-FRIENDLY GAMES & ACTIVITIES FOR LANGUAGE INSTRUCTION

GRADES 1 - 8

Debbie Hisam & Linda Seth

etc. publications

ACKNOWLEDGMENTS

The authors of Vocabulary GROWth would like to express our most sincere thanks to our families. They have allowed us the immense amount of time and concentration that it took to produce this wonderful project. Our families didn't seem to mind that we worked on this book at every opportunity, including between baseball innings, in the waiting room of the dentist's office, and in the car on the way to just about everywhere.

A special thank you goes to everyone who purchased our first book, GROW: Parts of Speech. You have confirmed our belief that we have valuable ideas to offer.

We are once again grateful to Mary Jane Helgren for her wonderful cover art.

Much appreciation is extended to Jean DeGaetano who has given us tremendous encouragement and guidance over the past few years. Our potential for success has been greatly increased by our long-distance friend's willingness to share her years of experience.

L. S. and D. H.

Printed in the U.S.A.

Printed by:
Easton Printing Co.
Parkersburg, WV

Books in this series:
GROW: Parts of Speech (1998)
Vocabulary GROWth (2000)

For more information or inquiries about workshops from etc. publications

RR 1 Box 24 A, Friendly, West Virginia 26146
e-mail: GROWetc@hotmail.com

INTRODUCTION

Vocabulary GROWth is a collection of activities designed for classroom teachers and specialists who teach and/or reinforce vocabulary skills. The activities included in this book are fun and interesting for both teachers and students, and they are definitely a break from normal classroom routine. Lessons are designed to be easily used by teachers who provide large or small group language intervention. Collaborative teaching becomes easy!

The target population for Vocabulary GROWth is generally first through eighth grades, but many high school resource classes could also benefit. Use of resource lists in the appendix will allow you to expand lessons and challenge students. Each activity is designed to involve every student.

When grouping students for team activities, do so as equitably as possible. This will result in better cooperative learning, and will encourage students to perform more competitively.

All necessary materials except regular classroom supplies, such as pencils and paper, are included in this book. Only a few pages will require duplication before using.

Most activities in this book can be easily adapted to a variety of game or non-game formats. Alternative methods for implementing each activity are suggested under MODIFICATIONS by narration and/or by symbols. The MODIFICATION SYMBOLS section of the book (pages vii - ix) gives complete explanations of each symbol.

Vocabulary GROWth lessons address many goals in addition to vocabulary development, such as auditory skills, cooperative teamwork, and analytical thinking. OBJECTIVES for each activity can be individually reviewed for more specific information.

The authors of this book feel strongly that there are many fun, nontraditional ways to be successful in the classroom without being tied to worksheets. This is the reason for the publication of Vocabulary GROWth.

TABLE OF

(Read below the title on each activity page a single sentence summary of the lesson.)

ANTONYMS / SYNONYMS

CATEGORIES / CLASSIFICATION

COMPOUND WORDS

CONTRACTIONS

HETERONYMS

HOMOPHONES

MULTIMEANING WORDS

*Indicates a duplicate listing

CONTENTS

(Read below the title on each activity page a single sentence summary of the lesson.)

*Indicates a duplicate listing

OBJECTIVES ADDRESSED

EXPLANATION	ABBREVIATION
* To improve understanding of ambiguity	Ambiguity
* To improve usage and understanding of antonyms	Antonyms
* To improve auditory association skills	Auditory association
* To improve auditory memory skills	Auditory memory
* To improve usage and understanding of base words	Base words
* To improve usage and understanding of categories	Categories
* To improve usage of classification skills	Classification
* To improve usage and understanding of compound words	Compounds
* To improve usage and understanding of contractions	Contractions
* To improve creative thinking	Creativity
* To improve usage and understanding of heteronyms	Heteronyms
* To improve usage and understanding of homophones	Homophones
* To improve usage and understanding of humor	Humor
* To improve usage of multimeaning words (homographs)	Multimeaning words
* To improve usage and understanding of plurals	Plurals
* To improve usage and understanding of prefixes	Prefixes
* To improve usage and understanding of relational vocabulary	Relationships
* To improve usage and understanding of rhyming words	Rhymes
* To improve sentence production	Sentences
* To improve usage of strategies for success	Strategies
* To improve usage and understanding of suffixes	Suffixes
* To improve usage and understanding of synonyms	Synonyms
* To improve teamwork and cooperation	Teamwork
* To improve analytical thinking	Thinking
* To improve vocabulary skills	Vocabulary

MODIFICATION SYMBOLS

Various game-playing or scoring formats may be substituted for specific activities. To see which substitutions might be appropriate check the icons pictured under each activity's MODIFICATIONS section.

RAISE YOUR CARDS: This response mode can be utilized to quickly and easily view all students' responses simultaneously. This format can be used only when the same 2 - 6 choices of responses are required each time.

Give each student the number cards he will need. On the chalkboard write the answer key for each number. For example, #1 means "synonym", #2 means "antonym"... When each student has selected one card to indicate his response, say "Raise your cards", and all students simultaneously do so. It is then easy to identify students who are having difficulty with the targeted concept. If desired, team points may be earned by individuals who respond correctly.

BEE: This format is that of a traditional spelling bee. Place two teams in lines facing each other, and alternate questions between them. Only the person whose turn it is may respond. If correct, he remains standing. If incorrect, he must sit down. The team with the last player (or the most players) left standing at the end of play is the winner.

CIRCLE BEE: Arrange students in a circle around the room. Announce that anyone who is wearing blue jeans (or anything else that is common to about one-half of the students) must sit down in his place on the circle. Choose any standing student to respond to a particular task. Continue searching for correct responses by choosing standing students in order around the circle. If a student's response is correct, he remains standing. If he is incorrect, he must sit down in his place. After all standing students have had a turn to respond, have all standing students sit and all sitting students stand. Choose a student to answer the first question and proceed as above. Playing in this fashion gives students who are having difficulty with a particular concept twice the number of chances to respond.

TICKETS: Divide the class into teams for a task. Choose one person from each team to be the respondent for the first question. Bring all respondents to the front of the class and give each three tickets (colored paper, token...). Remove one ticket from each respondent with each guess. When a student is out of tickets he may no longer guess. When the correct response is finally given, begin again, giving each new respondent three tickets. Team points may be awarded, if desired.

COOPERATIVE TEAMWORK: Students are divided into teams and given a task. After a team conference one student from each group records its answer and waits his turn to present the team's response. Team points may be awarded for correct responses.

⌘ TIC TAC TOE: (As a game playing modification) On the chalkboard draw a 3 x 3 (or 4 x 4) tic tac toe grid. Label each square with clues designed to elicit the targets, or with numbers which refer to a list of clues for the targets. Divide the class into two teams and alternate turns. If a student gives a correct response, he places his team's symbol ("X" or "O") in the appropriate square on the grid. The first team to earn three squares in a row horizontally, vertically, or diagonally wins the game.

TIC TAC TOE: (As a scoring modification) Divide the class into two teams and draw a 3 x 3 (or 4 x 4) tic tac toe grid on the chalkboard. Designate Team "X" and Team "O". Alternate teams asking for responses. Each time a student answers correctly, she may place her team's mark in the square of her choice. The first team to place 3 (or 4) of its marks in a row horizontally, vertically, or diagonally wins.

● DOT-TO-DOT: Use the dot-to-dot grid provided in the appendix or draw a similar one on the board. Assign each team a number and alternate asking questions. Each time a respondent is correct, he draws a connecting line between any two adjacent vertical or horizontal (not diagonal) dots on the grid. A player should attempt to put the fourth side on a connected-line square so that he may place his team's number inside the square. When time expires, the team with the most completed squares (the most numbers on the grid) is declared the winner. (Teammates may not tell players which two dots to connect.)

♌ FAST TRACK: On the chalkboard draw a racetrack with the same number of lanes as there are teams for the activity. Label each lane with a team number and divide each into the same number of "miles". Place each team's "car" (self-stick note or erasable "X") at the starting line. Alternate asking for responses from each team. Move a team's car into the next mile each time a correct response is given. The first car to reach the finish line wins.

♒ WATCH YOUR STEP: On the chalkboard draw a set of stairs. Place a self-stick note at the bottom of the steps for each participating team or assign each team a number and write it in chalk at the bottom of the stairs. Alternate asking for responses from teams. Each time a respondent is incorrect, move her team's marker up one step. Do not advance markers for correct responses. The first team to reach the top step topples over and loses. The team that is then closest to the bottom step wins.

✎ H-O-R-S-E: Divide the class into teams. Ask a question or assign a task to which the first person from each team must respond. Responses may be quickly written, or students may hold up number cards to indicate their answers. When all players are ready, ask for responses. If any team has the correct answer, all teams who do not have the correct answer earn one letter toward the spelling of a predetermined word, such as "SENTENCE". The game ends when any team spells the entire word. The team with the least number of letters wins. (NOTE: If no team answers correctly, no team earns a letter.)

FOOTBALL: Divide the class into two teams. On the chalkboard draw a football field with ten 10-yardline markings. Put one team's name on each end of the field. Use a magnet or self-stick note to represent the football and place it in the middle of the field. Alternate teams to elicite responses. For each correct response move the "ball" 10 yards closer to the answering team's goal. For each incorrect response, move back 10 yards. When a team reaches the goal line, tally six points and, if desired, allow the team to try for an extra point. Return the ball to the 50-yardline and begin again with the nonscoring team.

Two footballs, one for each team, may also be used.

BASEBALL: On the chalkboard draw a diamond-shaped playing field. Label the corners as "home", "1", "2", and "3". Choose dissimilar magnets or self-stick notes to represent each of the teams. Move these markers around the "playing field" as teammates give correct responses. Each time a team's marker lands on or passes "home", a run (one point) is scored. Questions may have up to four parts, such as "Name four words that rhyme with "spark". If correct, award four bases (homerun). If partially correct, award one base per correct component.

An alternate way to play would be to weight the questions by difficulty, stating ahead of time how many bases can be earned by a particular question.

CAPTURE THE FLAG: Divide the class into two teams. On the chalkboard draw a double set of ~~stairs leading~~ to a common top step. Make sure both sets of stairs have the same number of steps. Draw a flagpole with a flag on the top. Mark an "X" on each side of the stairs to represent each team. Alternate eliciting responses from each team, and with each correct response move the the team's "X" up one step. The first team to reach the flag wins. Return both flags to the bottom steps and begin again or allow the non-winning team to continue from its present position.

WRITING INDEPENDENTLY: Each student records his own response on paper. Team points may be awarded for correct responses, if desired.

ANSWERING ALOUD: Team or individual points may be awarded, if desired, when using this response mode. Responses may be written before being presented aloud.

SMALL GROUP MODIFICATIONS: Assign smaller numbers for each team, or let each person be her own team. Assign fewer teams than indicated in the activity procedures. Require fewer or more responses than the activity's procedure states.

...AND
AWAY
WE
GO!

SAME DIFFERENCE

Students will decide if word pairs are synonyms, antonyms or unrelated.

OBJECTIVES: Vocabulary
Antonyms, Synonyms
Auditory association
Relationships

TARGET POPULATION: Grades 2 & above
MATERIALS: Chalkboard & chalk
1, 2 & 3 cards (copy one/student from appendix)
Word Pair List (provided)

PROCEDURE: Give each student a 1 card, a 2 card and a 3 card. On the chalkboard write the following answer key for the cards:

1 = SYNONYM 2 = ANTONYM 3 = NEITHER

Instruct students that holding up a 1 card indicates that they have chosen "SYNONYM" as an answer, 2 means "ANTONYM", etc. Make sure that all students understand this correspondence by asking them to hold up the card that means "ANTONYM"... When students understand the correspondence begin the game.

Read to the class the first pair of words chosen from the provided list. Instruct students that they are to determine which word from the chalkboard correctly tells the relationship of the given words. For example, if the word pair is "large/big", students who understand the instructions and the vocabulary will prepare to hold up their 1 cards ("SYNONYM"). In order to prevent others from viewing his selection, each student holds his number card against his chest. The unused number cards should be turned face down on his desk.

When all students are ready say, "Raise your cards", and students do so simultaneously. No student is permitted to change his selection at this point. Explain answers to students who have responded incorrectly.

Continue the activity for as long as desired with additional word pairs from the provided list.

MODIFICATIONS: This activity may be played as a game by dividing the class into teams. Team points can be earned by each member who responds correctly, or by the spokesperson of the group who correctly reports its consensus. If individual players are scoring points for their teams, be certain that all teams have an equal number of players, or use "extra" players

as follows: 1) Let their correct responses add points to all teams' scores
2) Use them as "judges" of correct responses
3) Use them as scorekeepers

To eliminate the use of an answer key, a set of cards can be prepared which say "SYNONYM", "ANTONYM" and "NEITHER". Give a set of cards to each player or to one player from each team (for taking turns).

Word Pair List

(S = SYNONYM A = ANTONYM N = NEITHER)

A back/front
N doctor/healthy
N want/like
A allow/forbid
A victory/defeat
N careful/helpful
A omit/include
N believe/okay
S disappear/vanish
A inferior/superior
N weather/rain
N cheese/butter
S fierce/ferocious
S caution/warn
S tranquil/peaceful
N obey/listen
N branch/tree
N apple/pie
S necessary/essential
A maximum/minimum
A flimsy/solid
N break/bend
A deep/shallow
S dry/parched

N school/house
A beneficial/harmful
A interior/exterior
N foggy/overcast
A temporary/permanent
S answer/reply
S powerful/mighty
A absent/present
A accept/refuse
S genuine/real
S liberty/freedom
N wedding/ceremony
S imitate/copy
A exact/vague
A offense/defense
N mustard/relish
S scream/yell
S paste/glue
N garden/lawn
N tree/mushroom
A noisy/quiet
S hare/rabbit
N sleep/snore
A above/below

S choice/option
N stadium/players
N spring/summer
A common/rare
S detach/separate
N flood/water
S happen/occur
A sensible/ridiculous
N ring/bracelet
A dry/humid
S fiddle/violin
S bug/insect
S fiction/fantasy
A argue/agree
N piano/organ
A find/hide
A enemy/friend
S grasp/hold
N sandals/socks
S moist/damp
A serious/humorous
S fat/obese
S woods/forest
S brave/courageous

OPPOSING VIEWS

Students will replace one word of a given sentence with its opposite.

OBJECTIVES: Thinking
Antonyms
Vocabulary

TARGET POPULATION: Grades 2 & above
MATERIALS: Sentence List (provided)
Chalkboard & chalk

PROCEDURE: Divide students into teams. Remind them that many words, but not all, have opposites. The words "pig" and "candle", for example, do not have opposites, but "big" and "give" do. Explain that the sentence that will be read and written on the board will contain several words that have opposites. To earn a point for his team a player must repeat the given sentence with one change. The change must be the substitution of one of the original words with its opposite. For example, the sentence, "She will walk to the post office" could be changed to, "He will walk to the post office" or "She will run to the post office." The new sentence does not have to make perfect sense.

Write a sentence from the provided list on the board. The first player from Team 1 must give a correct response to earn one point for her team. If she is successful, cross the original word from the board and write its replacement above or below it. No other team may replace that word again. Go to the first player from Team 2 and ask her to replace a *different* word in the sentence to create another sentence with an opposite meaning. If she responds appropriately, award one point, cross the replaced word from the board, and write its opposite above it. Continue taking turns from team to team.

If a player answers incorrectly, and at least one more correct response remains, the next team's player continues with the same sentence. If he, too, is incorrect, it goes to the next team . . . until each team in succession is unable to make a correct change, or until a player correctly announces that no more changes are possible. This announcement also earns a player a point for her team. Reveal remaining correct answers, if any, that exist. When all correct substitutions have been revealed, read the new sentence with all of the replacement words.

Write a second sentence from the provided list on the board and continue the activity as described. Make sure that every student has the chance to answer before allowing anyone a second turn.

Continue the procedure for as long as time permits, and then total all points. The team with the most points wins.

MODIFICATIONS: After each team has provided one replacement word for a chosen sentence, reveal all possibilities, and then begin round two with a new sentence and a different team going first.

Award one point per letter of the replacement word.

Sentence List

(Sentences in parentheses show appropriate opposites. Other correct responses may exist, so evaluate all suggestions. If no opposite exists, a dotted line appears beneath the word.)

Her mother has black hair.
(His father hasn't white ---.)

Everybody loved the little kids.
(Nobody hated --- large adults.)

Grandpa started many jobs.
(Grandma finished few ---.)

Mom got dressed early.
(Dad --- undressed late.)

I did say good night to Jacob.
(You didn't --- bad day from ---.)

Few questions have been totally answered.
(Many answers haven't --- partially asked.)

None of the children are quiet.
(All --- --- grown-ups aren't noisy.)

This store closes at day's end.
(That --- opens --- night's start.)

The boy's room was very dirty.
(--- girl's ---- wasn't slightly clean.)

My best friend has a difficult job.
(Your worst enemy hasn't --- easy ---.)

Aunt Terry and my sister pushed it off.
(Uncle --- or your brother pulled --- on.)

Yes, Mr. Lynch can be mean sometimes.
(No, Mrs. --- can't --- kind always.)

Give this to my tame rabbit.
(Take that from your wild ---.)

Those ladies won't come here.
(These men will go there.)

Our daughter passed her last exam.
(Your son failed his first ---.)

Don't open that cheap liquid soap.
(Do close this expensive solid ---.)

He lost his newest round blocks.
(She found her oldest square ---.)

He is a strong leader.
(She isn't --- weak follower.)

BEE SENSIBLE

Students will supply a list of words that could complete a given sentence.

OBJECTIVES: Vocabulary
Auditory Memory
Synonyms, Sentences
Creativity

TARGET POPULATION: Grades 1 - 5
MATERIALS: Sentence List (provided)
Chalkboard & chalk

PROCEDURE: Divide the class into two teams. Instruct teams to line up on opposite sides of the room facing each other as in an old fashioned spelling bee. Read aloud a sentence from the provided list and, if desired, write it on the board. The first person from Team 1 repeats the sentence inserting into the blank one word, and *only one word*, that would correctly complete it. In the example "The mouse _____ across the room", an acceptable response would be "The mouse scurries across the room." If the suggested word creates a grammatically correct, meaningful sentence, the student remains standing. If a student suggests an inappropriate, ungrammatical, or previously used word, she must sit down where she had been standing.

Play then passes to the other team. The first player on that team states the same sentence, but inserts a different word, such as, "The mouse crept across the floor." Once a word has been used it may not be used again for the remainder of the activity. Students may be required to remember all words that have been used or assist them by writing them on the board. Elicit at least 8 - 10 different responses before moving on to a new sentence. Students will thus be encouraged, but not required, to think of synonyms of previously used words.

Round one is over when every player has had one turn. Count the number of students that remain standing on each team and enter that number as the team's score.

All students stand again and play is resumed by reading another sentence for students to complete. Remind everyone that any words used in previous rounds are not to be reused. To challenge all students as equitably as possible, do not begin at the front of the line each time.

Continue the activity until time expires. The team with the most accumulated points is the winner.

MODIFICATIONS: This activity can be played as a circle bee. (See instructions under "MODIFICATION SYMBOLS" on page vii.)

In grades 3 - 5 this activity can be done with teams of students working together to compile a list of words to complete a given sentence. After a specified amount of time, points are awarded for each correct word that *no other team* has on its list.

✍ ✋ ⌘ ● ♒ ⚑ ▭ ♌ ⚐ ❖

Sentence List

The mouse ____ across the room.
Mary sent her a ____.
The clown hugged the baby ____.
My parents always dance ____.
She created a wonderful ____.
The chicken walked ____ the fence.
Mom placed the ____ in the house.
The pup growled ____ at the bear.
Ms. Nelson ____ her hair.
His sick brother felt ____.
Dad loves his new red ____.
The rock star's pants were ____.
The sunshine made me feel ____.
Sammy swallowed six ____.
Marvin jogged around the ____.
I swatted at the annoying ____.
Three friends sat under the ____.
Harry felt ____ when he saw the smoke.
The band's song sounded ____.
I ____ better than you do.

THE SAME GAME

Students will replace a sentence's targeted word with a synonym.

OBJECTIVES: Vocabulary
Synonyms
Auditory memory

TARGET POPULATION: Grades 2 & above
MATERIALS: Sentence List (provided)
Chalkboard & chalk

PROCEDURE: Divide the class into teams and read them a sentence from the provided list. Identify the target word that is to be changed to a word with the same or very similar meaning. The first person from Team 1 will respond by attempting to repeat the sentence with that one modification. For example, if the original sentence is "All the way home we followed a shiny, black *vehicle*", the student's response might be "All the way home we followed a shiny, black *van.*" If his replacement word is indeed a synonym, or nearly a synonym, of the targeted word, he scores one point. Correct or not the first player from Team 2 now responds to the same sentence. Alternate teams and continue as described until at least two synonyms have been revealed. Allow each team up to two tries for each given sentence before revealing several correct possibilities and moving on to a new sentence.

Write the "used" responses on the board so that they will not be reused at any time during the remainder of the game. When writing the words on the board, group them in pairs if they are indeed synonyms, or write them on chart paper to be posted as a word bank for future creative writing assignments.

Continue playing until everyone has had a turn, or until time expires. Be sure that all teams have had an equal number of chances to earn points. The team with the most points at the end of play is the winner.

MODIFICATIONS: Award an extra point to any player who on his turn is successfully able to provide two synonyms for the sentence's targeted word.

Sentence List

	EXAMPLES
A child interrupted our conversation.	(toddler, youngster)
We saw a magnificent display of fireworks.	(superb, fantastic)
Last winter was frigid.	(freezing, glacial)
There were rats in the vacant dwelling.	(building, apartment)
The clergyman was at a meeting in Town Hall.	(minister, priest)
Dad brought us a darling puppy yesterday.	(cute, adorable)
His response came via e-mail.	(answer, reply)
Mom became anxious when she heard about the wreck.	(concerned, worried)
Jorge had a nightmare about a gigantic monster.	(huge, enormous)
Ned was horrified by the very thought of spiders.	(frightened, scared)
The weather was absolutely miserable yesterday.	(terrible, awful)
Santa Claus looks plump.	(chubby, fat)
This is the most current weather report.	(recent, up-to-date)
The two kittens like to frolic on the bed.	(play, romp)
Henry had a nasty gash on his leg.	(cut, laceration)
A phantom appeared in the old haunted house.	(spook, ghost)
The painting of his grandfather hung by the front door.	(portrait, picture)
She is always gratified by seeing her grandchildren.	(pleased, satisfied)
Wayne noisily munched some crackers.	(chewed, ate)
Gavin ate the entire pizza.	(whole, complete)
The floor covering was shaggy and green.	(rug, carpet)
The performance was quite uninteresting.	(dull, boring)
The girl shrieked when she burned herself.	(yelled, screamed)
Which portion of the book did you most enjoy?	(part, section)
His shirt got caught on the brambles.	(thorns, stickers)
Manny's timepiece had a dead battery.	(watch, clock)
The clothes dried quickly on that gusty afternoon.	(breezy, windy)
The basement seemed very humid.	(damp, moist)
Toss that ball to your brother.	(throw, fling)
Throw that rubbish into the barrel.	(trash, garbage)
Shawn glanced at the new girl.	(looked, peeked)
He is juvenile, even for a kindergartner.	(immature, young)
J.T. has a lot of knowledge about computers.	(information, facts)
Paolo flew down the highway in his new convertible.	(sped, raced)

RIGHT ON TARGET

Students will label three of four related words as "target", "antonym", "synonym", and "rhyme", and then write a word that fits the leftover label.

OBJECTIVES: Synonyms, Antonyms
Strategies
Rhymes
Thinking
Teamwork

TARGET POPULATION: Grades 4 & above
MATERIALS: Chalkboard & chalk
Target Word List (provided)
Paper & pencil/team
Label Cards (copy 1 set/team)

PROCEDURE: Divide the class into teams of 4. Assign extra players to teams as helpers, but they will not get a label card in the first round. Send each team to its own section of the room with a piece of paper and a pencil, and one each of the following label cards: "Antonym", "Synonym", "Rhyme", and "Target". Each member (except the extras) of each team takes any one of the label cards to start.

Begin the following chart on the chalkboard:

TARGET	SYNONYM	ANTONYM	RHYME
answer	________	question	dancer

Explain how each of the provided words relates to the target word. Then in a different place on the chalkboard write the *same* row of words as follows:

answer	question	dancer	_______
T	A	R	S

Note that the words listed above are from one line of the provided target list, but one word is randomly omitted, and the other three words have been rearranged. A blank line has been drawn to replace the omitted word. The capital letter under each word correlates to one of the label cards ("Dancer" is the Rhyme).

Allow each team to physically arrange itself in a line according to the label card that each player is holding. The order of the cards (players) should match the order of the words on the board. In the above example the order would be as follows: the target card, the antonym card, the rhyme card, and the synonym card.

After each team is in order the one member who holds the label card for the "blank" (the synonym card holder in the example above), writes one word on his team's paper to replace the blank (a synonym of the target word "answer").

Teammates may assist the cardholder in determining a word to write. While learning to play, however, accept oral suggestions and select one, such as "reply" or "respond", to complete the chart on the board. Written responses do not have to match the word from the provided list to be correct.

Erase the words on the board (not the chart). Choose another row of words from the provided list, randomly omit one, and write the other three on the board in any rearranged order. To prevent copying tell players to switch label cards so that other teams do not know which card anyone holds. Then instruct teams to determine the labels that correlate with the words on the board, and to arrange themselves in the correct order. Remind teams that its member who is holding the label card for the "blank" must write one word to replace that "blank".

When a sufficient amount of time has passed or when most teams are ready announce, "Time". No more arranging or writing may be done for this round.

Determine with student assistance the correct label for each word. Write the first letter of the label under each of the words. Then say, "Turn your cards", and all members of all teams display them simultaneously. Award each team two points if all of its team members are lined up in the correct order. Award an extra point to any team that wrote a word that correctly replaces the blank. Fill in the chart on the board with the three given words and any correct fill-in.

Instruct teammates to again exchange label cards. Extra players who did not hold a card in round one should get one now. Repeat the above process.

Continue for as long as time allows, and then declare the team with the most points to be the winner.

MODIFICATIONS: Allow teams to earn bonus points if they can list several appropriate words to complete blanks.

With small groups, allow partners or individuals to arrange label cards on their desktops. Award points for the correct arrangement of the label cards, and for completing the blank appropriately.

Word List

TARGET	SYNONYM	ANTONYM	RHYME
answer	reply	question	dancer
blank	empty	filled	thank
buy	purchase	sell	try
brave	fearless	cowardly	shave
alone	solitary	together	cologne
near	close	far	cheer
shy	coy	outspoken	sky
dense	thick	thin	fence
simple	easy	difficult	dimple
quick	fast	slow	thick
grief	sorrow	happiness	chief
tardy	late	early	hardy
mend	repair	break	blend
often	frequently	seldom	coffin
piece	part	whole	crease
recall	remember	forget	football
vague	unclear	exact	Craig
fair	equitable	unreasonable	chair
wise	smart	stupid	guys
snug	tight	loose	hug
doubt	question	believe	shout
bold	assertive	timid	gold
complex	complicated	simple	convex
evil	vile	good	weevil
stable	sturdy	flimsy	label
foe	enemy	friend	know
cruel	mean	kind	jewel
cheerful	happy	somber	tearful
allow	permit	forbid	avow
serene	calm	chaotic	marine
recent	modern	ancient	decent
petty	trivial	important	Betty

TARGET
ANTONYM
SYNONYM
RHYME

SYNONYM FLAVORED SCRAMBLED EGGS

Students will unscramble a word when given a synonym clue.

OBJECTIVES: Synonyms
Vocabulary
Thinking
Strategies

TARGET POPULATION: Grades 3 & above
MATERIALS: Secret Word List (provided)
Tickets (copy 3/team from appendix)
Chalkboard & chalk
Clock with second hand (optional)

PROCEDURE: Divide the class into teams. Have one player from each team go to the front of the room to play round one. Give each of the standing players three tickets that she may spend to make guesses. On the chalkboard write the first scrambled secret word. If any of the standing students wants to take a guess as to the identity of the secret word, she must spend one ticket to do so.

Choose the first standing player to raise her hand. If the player correctly guesses the secret word, she earns 3 points for her team. If, after 10 - 15 seconds, no one wishes to guess (or to guess again) reveal the first letter of the secret word. Choose the first ticket holder to raise her hand, but again she must spend one ticket. A correct guess after one clue earns 2 points.

If no one is correct, or no guess is taken, reveal the synonym clue for the secret word. A correct guess now earns 1 point. At each stage of each round, allow any or all of the standing students to guess, as long as each respondent has a ticket to spend.

Anytime after the first letter of the response has been revealed, a standing student may elect to spend a ticket for a 15-second consultation with her teammates. Teammates are not permitted to request the consultation. Conferring should be done quietly so that other teams cannot overhear the discussion. Another ticket must be spent for a player to guess the secret word after a team consultation. It is permissible, however, for any other ticket holder to guess even while a team is conferring.

If no one is able to correctly guess the secret word after all clues have been given, reveal it. Begin the next round by choosing a new player from each team to go to the front of the room. Give each of these players three tickets and write a new scrambled word on the board. Continue as in round one.

When everyone has had one chance to be a standing player, count the points earned by each team. The team with the most points wins.

MODIFICATIONS: Do not allow tickets to be spent for team consultations.

✋ ❄ ♒ ⚐ ❖ ♌ ⌘ ✍ ● ✌

Secret Word List

Scrambled letters:	(3 points)	YRRLAE	OEGVL	TIFHG
First letter:	(2 points)	R	G	F
Synonym clue:	(1 point)	infrequently	mitten	battle
Secret word:	....	(RARELY)	(GLOVE)	(FIGHT)

LRRUE	LYEHHTA	SPNAT	DLROW	TRESO
R	H	P	W	S
yardstick	well	trousers	earth	shop
(RULER)	(HEALTHY)	(PANTS)	(WORLD)	(STORE)
EALFM	KNEAS	TSBAL	RHAST	AELVS
F	S	B	T	S
fire	serpent	explosion	junk	servant
(FLAME)	(SNAKE)	(BLAST)	(TRASH)	(SLAVE)
AREMCS	TRALEPT	HFIET	INAMTONU	IENCCHK
S	P	T	M	C
yell	tray	robber	hill	poultry
(SCREAM)	(PLATTER)	(THIEF)	(MOUNTAIN)	(CHICKEN)
YTROS	THAOSCM	YNCDA	TRAPCE	HAHOOTPPRG
S	S	C	C	P
tale	tummy	sweets	rug	picture
(STORY)	(STOMACH)	(CANDY)	(CARPET)	(PHOTOGRAPH)
MESLI	TBIARB	CCOHU	GLENAS	TMTUERP
S	R	C	A	T
grin	hare	sofa	guardians	horn
(SMILE)	(RABBIT)	(COUCH)	(ANGELS)	(TRUMPET)

TARGET PRACTICE

Students will guess a target word when given an antonym, a synonym, and a rhyming word.

OBJECTIVES: Synonyms, Antonyms
Rhymes, Thinking
Teamwork, Strategies
Vocabulary, Relationships

TARGET POPULATION: Grades 3 & above
MATERIALS: Chalkboard & chalk
Target Word List (provided)
Tickets (copy 3/team from appendix)

PROCEDURE: Divide the class into teams of 3 or 4 and assign each a spokesperson for round one. Give each spokesperson 3 tickets that are necessary for buying guesses.

On the chalkboard write the following three words: synonym, antonym, rhyme. Make sure that students know the meanings of these words by providing several examples.

From the provided word list select a target word for teams to guess. Do <u>not</u> reveal the target word, but select one of the other three associated words (antonym, synonym, or rhyme), to write on the board. Do <u>not</u> tell students whether the written word is the antonym, synonym, or rhyme. Teams must figure that out for themselves. Allow a short period of time for teammates to discuss some possible target words. For example, if the written word is "brainy", it may be a synonym for the target word "intelligent", an antonym for "stupid", or a rhyme for "zany".

If any team chooses to take a guess as to the identity of the target word, the team's spokesperson after team consultation and approval raises his hand with a ticket in it. He shows his ticket to prove that he is eligible to respond. At this point, however, only a little information has been given, and a team's guess will truly be a guess. After all spokespersons who wish to guess have done so, write another word from the associated target word list on the board. This word will provide an additional clue to the missing target word. For example, the next written word may be "drizzly". Teams now confer to try to figure out the target word based on the two clues, "brainy" and "drizzly". After all guesses have been made for this clue, reveal the final one. Again allow consultation time and accept guesses from ticket holders. Reveal the target word, if no team is able to do so.

A team earns points when its spokesperson correctly announces the target word. If the word is guessed after the first clue, 3 points are earned.

After two clues award 2 points. If the word is guessed after the final clue, the team scores 1 point.

For each clue a spokesperson may guess as many times as his team directs him, provided he has a ticket to spend for each guess. When a spokesperson is out of tickets he is finished.

Change spokespersons and begin again with a clue associated with another target word. Do not present the clues in the same order as in the previous round.

MODIFICATIONS: Award an extra point to any team that guesses the target word when it spends its *first* ticket.

Word List

TARGET	Antonym	Synonym	Rhyme	TARGET	Antonym	Synonym	Rhyme
FIND	lose	locate	kind	CHEAP	expensive	inexpensive	deep
DRY	wet	arid	cry	SICK	healthy	ill	brick
WALK	run	stroll	talk	CURLY	straight	wavy	early
CLEAN	dirty	spotless	bean	RAINY	clear	drizzly	brainy
SPICED	bland	flavorful	priced	RUN	walk	jog	stun
WEAK	strong	feeble	cheek	BOY	girl	lad	toy
ROUND	square	circular	pound	HILLY	flat	mountainous	silly
RICH	poor	wealthy	pitch	BLACK	white	dark	slack
BAD	good	evil	glad	COLD	hot	chilly	mold
AWAKE	asleep	alert	shake	SMILE	frown	grin	style
STOP	continue	halt	mop	PULL	push	tug	full
BEST	worst	ultimate	chest	CHEERFUL	grouchy	happy	tearful
ODD	common	unusual	prod	FAT	skinny	obese	brat
SCREAM	whisper	yell	dream	REPAIR	break	fix	beware
EQUAL	different	alike	sequel	MESSY	tidy	sloppy	dressy
GREEDY	generous	selfish	weedy	GLOOMY	merry	sorrowful	roomy
HOARSE	clear	husky	coarse	QUIET	noisy	silent	riot
POLITE	rude	mannerly	tonight	CHUCKLE	cry	laugh	buckle
OCEAN	desert	sea	lotion	GRAND	humble	splendid	land
MUDDY	clear	murky	buddy	BUILD	demolish	construct	spilled
SCRATCH	itch	scrape	latch	HARD	simple	difficult	charred

ANTBALL

Students will add prefixes to words in a given sentence in order to create opposite meanings.

OBJECTIVES: Antonyms
Prefixes
Vocabulary, Teamwork
Auditory Association & memory

TARGET POPULATION: Grades 4 & above
MATERIALS: Sentence List (provided)
Chalk & chalkboard
Magnet or self-stick note

PROCEDURE: Divide the class into two teams. On the chalkboard draw a football field with 10 ten-yardline markings. Put one team's name on each end of the field. Use a magnet or self-stick note to represent the football, and place it in the middle of the field (50-yardline) to begin.

On the chalkboard write the following prefixes and tell students that each has the capability of making opposites of base words:

un- dis- mis- il- im- in- ir- de- non-

For the first sentence choose a "squad" (three students) from Team 1 to work together without help from other teammates. Do the same for Team 2. Appoint a "captain" (spokesperson) for each squad.

Read a sentence from the provided list. Allow each squad about 30 seconds to find <u>two</u> words within the sentence that can be changed to their opposites by adding one of the given prefixes. (NOTE: Two words within the sentence will become opposite, but the entire sentence may not have an opposite meaning.)

When time expires ask Team 1's squad to state <u>one</u> of its answers. Team 1's response, if correct, will include a given prefix attached to one of the original words from the provided sentence. The new word must be the grammatically correct opposite of the original word. For example, "unhappy" would be a correct response, but "dishappy" and "dehappy" cannot be found in a dictionary. If Team 1 gives a correct response, move the "football" ten yards closer to its goal and ask Team 2 for the second response for that sentence. If Team 1 is incorrect, a "fumble" has occurred which allows Team 2 to attempt the same word with a different prefix, or a different word from the same sentence. If Team 2 is correct, move the football ten yards closer to its goal. If

they fumble, allow Team 1 to give one more response. Allow no more thinking time before this response is given. If one of the targeted words remains unrevealed at this point, allow Team 2 a second attempt.

If either or both of the correct responses in a sentence are still unidentified after each team has had two turns, write the target words on the board. Then ask the class to volunteer the correct responses, but do not move the football.

Allow these same squads to repeat the above procedure with a second sentence. Begin with the team that did not have the last correct response. Follow the same procedure with this sentence, and then choose a new squad from each team. Repeat the procedure until all students have been on a squad at least once. If time allows, regroup students into new squads so that they must work with different teammates.

A team scores a touchdown when the football advances to the opponent's goal line (0 yardline). Award the team 6 points, and allow them to try for an extra point. Give them 30 seconds to name three other words that begin with the same prefix as the one they used to earn their last yardage. Words already used during the activity may not be reused. For example, if a scoring team identified the word "happy", and changed it to "unhappy" to score a touchdown, the captain might earn an extra point by stating the words "unbelievable", "undo", and "uncomplicated". All three words must be correct to earn the bonus.

If time allows, return the ball to the 50-yardline and begin again. The team that just scored will not go first.

When time expires, the team with the highest score wins.

MODIFICATIONS: Use two "footballs" and have each team move its own toward the opponent's goal in order to score.

Sentence List

Lee must cover his invention to magnetize some of its parts. (uncover, demagnetize)
I agree with you because I know your facts are accurate. (disagree, inaccurate)
In some countries it is legal to dress in front of others. (illegal, undress)
The bullet was lodged in his hip, but his condition was stable. (dislodged, unstable)
He waited patiently for the boy to twist the line for the kite. (impatiently, untwist)
Claire gave several logical and rational answers to the teacher. (illogical, irrational)
The admiral is capable of activating a nuclear device. (incapable, deactivating)
Did the friendly doctor diagnosis your problem? (unfriendly, misdiagnose)
She willingly took notes at the regular meeting. (unwillingly, irregular)
He said the formal paperwork for the project was complete. (informal, incomplete)
The spy coded that message properly. (decoded, improperly)
The mature child was pleasant to all of them. (immature, unpleasant)
Dairy products are supposed to be healthy for you. (non-dairy, unhealthy)
My cold appeared, so I took the correct dosage of medicine. (disappeared, incorrect)
I think it was possible for him to do the damage. (impossible, undo)
It was selfish of you to fog the truck's windshield. (unselfish, defog)
Because he is responsible, let Pedro tie the cable. (irresponsible, untie)
Only fiction writers are eligible for the prize. (nonfiction, ineligible)
An operator connected her after she had dialed twice. (disconnected, misdialed)
The honest banker printed the schedules. (dishonest, misprinted)
The gun fired as the violent grizzly came closer. (misfired, nonviolent)
The educated teenager behaved during the lecture. (uneducated, misbehaved)
We sold an even number of perfect books. (uneven, imperfect)
The judge was partial, but he thought my ideas made sense. (impartial, nonsense)
That living plant was well hydrated. (nonliving, dehydrated)
I read the part about keeping the flower protected. (misread, unprotected)

AN OPEN & SHUT CASE

Students will listen to a sentence and identify the two words that sometimes have opposite meanings.

OBJECTIVES: Antonyms
Auditory association & memory
Vocabulary, Thinking

TARGET POPULATION: Grades 2 & above
MATERIALS: Sentence List (provided)

PROCEDURE: Divide students into two teams and place them in two lines facing each other as in a traditional spelling bee. Tell students to raise their hands as soon as they can identify the two words in the given sentence that in some instances have opposite meanings.

Stand where it is easy to see who raises her hand first, and read the first sentence. Require the first hand-raiser to give an immediate response. If the response is correct, the student sits on the floor where she has been standing. The object of the game is to be the first team to have all members sitting. If the responding player is incorrect, or does not answer immediately, reread the sentence *for the opposing team,* and ask for a response from the first person to raise her hand. Continue alternating teams until a correct response is given for that sentence, or until each team has had two tries.

Read the second sentence and again call on the first person from *either* team to raise her hand. If a sitting student tries to assist a teammate, or blurts out a response, she must again join the ranks of the standing.

Continue reading sentences and accepting answers until time expires, or until an entire team is seated. The team with all (or the most) players seated wins. Begin again, if time allows.

MODIFICATIONS: If seated students are not paying attention, require them to stand again.

State a pair of antonyms, or only one word of a pair, and require responding students to use both words in *one* meaningful sentence.

Sentence List

(The target words *as used in these sentences* may not be opposites, but they can be used as opposites in other contexts.)

The late Dr. King always woke up early every morning. (late/early)
I used the mop to dry the floor where it was wet from the ice. (wet/dry)
Mexico City is the capitol of the country of Mexico. (city/country)
Please put the shovel in the shed when you go out. (in/out)
The sun rose in the east as he walked down West 32nd Street. (east/west)
Kim will stay home with the puppies when we go to the store. (stay/go)
Unless I'm wrong, his office is down the hall on the right. (wrong/right)
That coat is too big for that little freckle-faced girl. (big/little)
Is it true that Latoya is wearing false eyelashes? (true/false)
The water from that old well made them sick. (well/sick)
If you'll lead the way to the barn, the horses will follow. (lead/follow)
His white shirt already had stains and black smudges on it. (black/white)
You'll find that it is easier to lose weight if you exercise. (find/lose)
She has always wondered why he never takes his hat off. (always/never)
Dear old Mrs. Carver gave me a brand new watch for my birthday. (old/new)
After being in the hot sun all day, I needed a cold drink. (hot/cold)
My baby brother likes to float his plastic fish in the kitchen sink. (float/sink)
I'll wear my low shoes when we go hiking in the high country. (high/low)
It was sweet of her to feed those sour apples to the horses. (sweet/sour)
The famous Spanish author was almost unknown in England. (famous/unknown)
Apologizing won't do you any good, unless you mend your evil ways. (good/evil)
Will Jonas be safe crossing that dangerous intersection alone? (safe/dangerous)
My friend told me that his worst enemy was back in town. (friend/enemy)
Dad tried to quiet the noisy baby, but he couldn't. (quiet/noisy)
We went through the front door and down the back hallway. (front/back)
I'll look you up when I come down to Texas. (up/down)
The best man gave the worst toast I've ever heard. (best/worst)
Before you start your homework, please go after the dog. (before/after)
The idea for her curly hair-do came straight from a magazine. (curly/straight)
Reuben turned on a light in the dark living room. (light/dark)
That rich cheesecake is a poor choice for a person on a diet. (rich/poor)
Sign your name at the bottom of the paper on top of that pile. (bottom/top)
Mr. Wu lost a temporary filling from a permanent tooth. (temporary/permanent)
That short math assignment was due a long time ago. (short/long)
This light fixture is too heavy for me to carry upstairs. (light/heavy)

The sun rose above the trees and shone on the valley below. (above/below)
Brent lost the ticket that proves he won the lottery. (lost/won)
He knew right away that I had the wrong tickets. (right/wrong)
Did you look for your coat in the lost and found department? (lost/found)
Sven told him to help her with the luggage. (him/her)
She loves tomato soup, but she says she hates tomatoes! (loves/hates)
Her hair was too long, and her skirt was too short to please Granny. (long/short)
I noticed that man in the front row sitting by a very tall woman. (man/woman)
None of those kids spent all of their money. (none/all)
We sang some pretty cool songs as we sat around the warm hearth. (cool/warm)
The shallow end of the pool is not deep enough for diving. (shallow/deep)
Mike likes to drive through the state park at dusk. (drive/park)
Push open that closet door and pull out my suitcase. (push/pull)
Would you show us the deer hide that your uncle has? (show/hide)
We mopped the floor and dusted the ceiling fan. (floor/ceiling)
If you catch a fly ball, throw it to first base. (catch/throw)
It's not hard to blend the sugar with the soft butter. (hard/soft)
When Emma is nervous she likes to watch the calm lake waters. (nervous/calm)
Wyatt has gotten so tall that all of his jeans are now too short. (tall/short)
Let's take a break, and I'll fix some hot chocolate for us. (break/fix)
His brother, Rocky, is really a smooth dancer. (rocky/smooth)
Everyone knows that nobody could do a better job. (everyone/nobody)
All of the imprisoned men received free counseling services. (imprisoned/free)
The formal invitation stated that casual attire was acceptable. (formal/casual)
Dad said he broke that spring when he was driving around last fall. (spring/fall)
I've thought it over and decided to place you under my supervision. (over/under)

QUICK PICKS

Students will guess "hink pinks" (pairs of rhyming words) after hearing their definitions.

OBJECTIVES: Vocabulary
Rhymes
Synonyms

TARGET POPULATION: Grades 3 & above
MATERIALS: Hink Pink Definitions (provided)
Chalkboard & chalk
[1] - [6] cards (copy one set/team plus one set/teacher from appendix)

PROCEDURE: Divide students into teams of up to six players each. Shuffle one set of number cards 1 - 6 (or 1 - 5 if there is a maximum of 5 players per team...) and pass them out to players from Team 1. Shuffle the other sets and deal them out to each of the other teams. Each team will, therefore, have one player with a [1] card, one player with a [2] card... If teams do not have equal numbers of players, give one player from each of the "shorted" teams two different number cards. In this case, when round one is finished, select different students to hold two number cards.

Shuffle the teacher number cards and randomly draw one. Announce the drawn number to the class. Anyone who is holding that number, one person from each team, must stand. Only those who are standing may respond to the first question. Sitting students may not assist their teammates.

Explain to standing students that a brief definition will be given. Students are to think of a hink pink (a pair of rhyming words) that fits the definition. Call on students in the order that they raise their hands. Students who respond incorrectly do not get another try for that definition.

State a definition from the provided list for one of the hink pinks and, if desired, write it on the board. Ask for a response from the first standing person who raises his hand. If his answer is correct, award his team two points. If he is incorrect, tell the other respondents one of two things: 1) that neither part of the given answer was correct; or 2) that one of the words (don't tell which one) in the student's answer was correct. Of the remaining standing students select the next to raise his hand. Ask for his response to the same definition. If he, too, is incorrect, tell if any part of his answer was right.

After two standing players have incorrectly attempted an answer, give the others a clue, but award only one point for a correct response. The clue given should be a word that rhymes with the hink pink pair. For example, if students are unable to guess "fat rat" from the definition "plump rodent", provide them with a rhyming word for the hink pink, such as "hat". If none of the standing students is able to come up with the correct hink pink, ask for a volunteer from the class to respond, but award no points.

Choose another number from the teacher's pile of cards so that new respondents will stand. Do not put any previously picked numbers back in the drawing until all have been selected. After all numbers have been called, collect each team's set, shuffle them, and redeal. Each student will now have a good chance of competing against a different group of students. Continue the activity for as long as time allows and then total all points. The team with the most points is the winner.

MODIFICATIONS: ⌘ ⚐ ⚐ ♒ ♌ ✌ ❖ ● ✋

Hink Pink Definitions

Police boss - TOP COP
Plump rodent - FAT RAT
Unkind adolescent - MEAN TEEN
Noontime drink - LUNCH PUNCH
Footwear watch - SOCK CLOCK
Little bouncing toy - SMALL BALL
Greasy fowl - SLICK CHICK
Dirty pal - MUDDY BUDDY
Ten-ton car - HEAVY CHEVY
Impartial grizzly - FAIR BEAR
Wet hobo - DAMP TRAMP
Seafood platter - FISH DISH
Tough security officer - HARD GUARD
Female's hair wave - GIRL'S CURLS
Shower for a king's son - PRINCE RINSE
Minister instructor - PREACHER TEACHER
Cozy carpet - SNUG RUG
Wheel in flames - TIRE FIRE
Artificial cobra - FAKE SNAKE
Correct tallness - RIGHT HEIGHT
Orderly chair - NEAT SEAT
Ill hen - SICK CHICK
Strange facial hair - WEIRD BEARD
Messy imitation - SLOPPY COPY
Doggie kiss - POOCH SMOOCH
Equine path - HORSE COURSE
Flower song - PLANT CHANT
Banana-colored man - YELLOW FELLOW
Clever pie - SMART TART
Stone's container - ROCK'S BOX
Cleaning tool store - MOP SHOP
University info - COLLEGE KNOWLEDGE
Money in the bank - CASH STASH
Tortoise squeezer - TURTLE GIRDLE
Cow fight - CATTLE BATTLE
Icy hammer - COOL TOOL
Great country - GRAND LAND
Ridiculous William - SILLY WILLY/BILLY
Wash finger marks - RINSE PRINTS
Lunar melody - MOON TUNE
Intelligent valentine - SMART HEART
Final explosion - LAST BLAST
Smashed cap - FLAT HAT
Pokey deer - SLOW DOE
Stinker's beds - SKUNK'S BUNKS
Sea-water cream - OCEAN LOTION

THINK HINK PINKS

Students will state a "hink pink" (pair of rhyming words) that fits a given definition.

OBJECTIVES: Rhyming, Vocabulary
Synonyms, Thinking
Teamwork

TARGET POPULATION: Grades 3 & above
MATERIALS: Pencil & paper/team
Chalkboard & chalk
Hink Pink Definitions (provided)

Flower Power

PROCEDURE: Divide the class into teams of 3 - 5 students and give each team's designated recorder a pencil and paper.

Write three hink pink definitions from the provided list on the chalkboard or have three prewritten definitions on a piece of paper that can be hung where everyone can see it. Explain to students that a hink pink is a pair of rhyming words, such as "fat cat" or "mad dad". Each team will be trying to solve all three of the given definitions in the given amount of time.

While teams are working on this set of three definitions, write the next three on another piece of paper, or in another place on the board to reduce delays for subsequent rounds of play. Cover these definitions to prevent teams from working ahead.

Tell each recorder to write one response for each definition and to stand when his team has completed all three. After a sufficient amount of time expires, *or when half of the teams have finished* announce, "Pencils down".

Read definition #1 and ask any recorder for the response that his team has written. If necessary, continue asking other recorders until the correct hink pink is revealed. Once identified, ask each team if its written response was correct. If at least one team has written the correct answer, tell each of the teams who were incorrect that they have earned the letter "H". On the chalkboard under team numbers record those H's as earned. The object of this game is to NOT earn letters on the board. Each time any team answers correctly, teams without correct responses earn one more letter toward the spelling of "HINK PINK". If any team spells "HINK PINK" in its entirety, the game is over and the team with the fewest letters wins.

If it happens that *no* team records a correct response for a particular definition, then *no* team is given a letter on the board. At least one team must get it right before the others are penalized.

Check the other hink pink responses, and then post the next three definitions. Change recorders, if desired, and continue playing as described. When one game is finished begin again, if time allows.

MODIFICATIONS: When only one team has the correct response, give the recorder for that team the option of adding one letter to each of the other teams or removing one letter from his own team.

Hink Pink Definitions

Devilish sailor - DEMON SEAMAN
Chilly pond - COOL POOL
Python dessert - SNAKE CAKE
Chubby feline - FAT CAT
Quick history - FAST PAST
Innovative footwear - NEW SHOE
Iron pot - METAL KETTLE
Library corner - BOOK NOOK
Paris park seat - FRENCH BENCH
Noisy fog - LOUD CLOUD
Ruler's jewelry - KING'S RINGS
Stingy crab - SELFISH SHELLFISH
Snail-like insect - SLUG BUG
Prison path - JAIL TRAIL
Postage winner - STAMP CHAMP
Feline taxi driver - TABBY CABBY
Big boat - LARGE BARGE
Boiling kettle - HOT POT
Lengthy tune - LONG SONG
Ancient metal - OLD GOLD
Enjoyable jog - FUN RUN
Fat newlywed - WIDE BRIDE
Hilarious cash - FUNNY MONEY
Sofa grump - COUCH GROUCH
White fingertip - PALE NAIL
Best dad - TOP POP

Curly dog scribble - POODLE DOODLE
Wise beginning - SMART START
Center violin - MIDDLE FIDDLE
Evening illumination - NIGHT LIGHT
Insect's trousers - ANT'S PANTS
Plant strength - FLOWER POWER
Sky noise mistake - THUNDER BLUNDER
King's wicked wife - MEAN QUEEN
Insect medicine - BUG DRUG
Meal group - LUNCH BUNCH
Primary ache - MAIN PAIN
Quick explosion - FAST BLAST
Happy parent - GLAD DAD
Police store - COP SHOP
Fine musical group - GRAND BAND
Tired flower - LAZY DAISY
Hog dance - PIG JIG
Bag pile - SACK STACK
Crazy kid - WILD CHILD
Beautiful town - PRETTY CITY
Cold capsule - CHILL PILL
Damp animal buddy - WET PET
Creek dweller - RIVER LIVER
Hung-up vehicle - STUCK TRUCK
Supper champ - DINNER WINNER
Someone else's mom - ANOTHER MOTHER

THINK FAST

Teammates in 60 seconds will name all the items that they can to fit a given category.

OBJECTIVES: Vocabulary,
Strategies, Categories
Auditory memory

TARGET POPULATION: Grades 1 & above
MATERIALS: Category List (provided)
Watch w/ second hand or one-minute timer
Chalkboard & chalk

PROCEDURE: Divide students into three or four teams. Begin with Team 1 and ask the first person to choose a number from 1 - 20. Locate the selected number on the provided category list and choose the best selection for the ability level of the playing team. Announce the category to Team 1 and say, "Go". Players from this team, in the manner described below, will then have just 60 seconds to name as many items as they can to fit the given category.

The first player from Team 1 must *correctly* name one item that suits the category before the second player from that team is allowed to respond. The second player must respond correctly before the third player gets a chance... No player is allowed to name an item out of turn, or to help another player. Tally one point for the team as each correct response is given. After all players on the team in rotation have successfully named one item, player number 1 responds again, and play continues as described until 60 seconds expire. Then ask the rest of the class for a few additional responses that would also fit the category, but award no points. (Suggestion: If a teammate says an answer out of turn, do not allow that word to be used for points by any player. If a player from another team calls out a response, the playing team may use it.)

Play continues in this fashion with the first player from Team 2 choosing a number from 1 - 20. Follow the same procedure with each team. When every team has used its 60 seconds to categorize and earn points, begin the next round by starting again with Team 1. The player who goes first in this round is the player who was due to respond in the previous round when time expired. This is also the player who selects the next number from 1 - 20.

Continue with as many rounds as time allows, making sure that each team has an equal number of chances to respond. Total all points when finished. The team with the most is the winner.

MODIFICATIONS: For smaller classes allow each player to function as his own team and list as many responses as possible within 60 seconds, or play as follows: Have the first person (or the only person) *from each team* respond in rotation to each category selected. Point in rotation to each standing player. Allow 5 seconds for a player to respond before pointing to the standing player from the next team. Do not wait for a correct response before moving on. Continue in rotation until 60 seconds expire. Begin the next category with the team that follows the last team to give a *correct* response.

✋ ✍ ❄ ❖ ♈

Category List

#	Easier	More Difficult	Most Difficult
1	holidays	things with a switch	pronouns
2	furniture	foods we eat raw	multiples of 7
3	fruits	things we do with our feet	states
4	TV programs	kinds of dogs	school subjects
5	round things	non-cartoon movies	religions
6	flowers	countries	fish
7	trees	cities	hobbies
8	insects	musical instruments	adjectives
9	kitchen things	sports team names	universities
10	drinks	things seen at a circus	spicy foods
11	cold things	capitols	languages
12	desserts	underwater things	card games
13	parts of the body	presidents of the U.S.A.	parts of a book
14	pets	indoor games	things we roll up
15	soft things	superheroes	words starting with "z"
16	hot things	cartoon characters	adverbs
17	birds	first words in questions	things sold in a jar
18	tools	math words	nursery rhymes
19	teachers in our school	things with buttons	gemstones
20	vehicles	restaurants	kinds of boats

SMART START

Students will name items that fit a given category when the beginning letter is provided.

OBJECTIVES: Categories
Vocabulary, Strategies
Teamwork, Creativity

TARGET POPULATION: Grades 2 & above
MATERIALS: Pencils and paper/team
Chalkboard & chalk
Category Suggestions (provided)

PROCEDURE: Divide the class into teams and select a recorder for each. Give each recorder paper and pencil, and instruct him to write a given category word down the left edge of his paper. Each recorder, for example, may be told to write the following:

S
P
O
R
T
S

It is then the responsibility of each team to think of one appropriate word that begins with each letter of the given category. Each new word must actually fit the selected category. Recorders will write their teams' selections horizontally on their papers using each letter of the vertical word as the first letter of their chosen response. When teams have finished or when a sufficient amount of time has passed announce, "Pencils down." In the above example a team's responses may be as follows:

Soccer		Softball
Ping-Pong		Powder Puff Football
Olympics	or	Olympics
Rowing		Rodeo
Tennis		Track
Swimming		Sailing

Ask each recorder to announce his team's written response to the first letter of the category. Any team that correctly selects a word that fits the category and begins with the specified letter earns one point if, *and only if*, no other team has chosen the same word.

Continue by asking for words that begin with the second letter of the given category, and so on. When all words for the entire category have been revealed, and all scores have been tallied, choose a new category. Select new recorders for each team, if desired, and proceed as described.

Instruct students that once a word has been used, it may not be used again for the remainder of the activity. When a letter occurs twice in one category title, as does the "S" in "SPORTS", score all the "S" words at the same time. Eliminate from all lists any duplicated words, no matter which "S" they were written beside. Continue the activity with as many rounds as desired and then total all scores. The team with the most points wins.

MODIFICATIONS: ✍ ❖ ♌ ✌

Category Suggestions

SPORTS	CLOTHES	MOVIES	GAMES
TOYS	JOBS	CITIES	FRUITS
COLORS	ANIMALS	STORES	DRINKS
CARS	FLOWERS	BUGS	GIRLS
	SNACKS	BOYS	

THE GUESSED LIST

Teams will list words that fit a given category and challenge other teams to reproduce the list.

OBJECTIVES: Categories, Vocabulary
Creativity
Teamwork

TARGET POPULATION: Grades 1 & above
MATERIALS: Paper & pencil/team
Categories List (provided)

PROCEDURE: Divide students into teams and designate a recorder for each. Give each recorder paper and pencil.

Select a category that suits the grade level, such as "kinds of trees", and announce it to Team 1. Select another category, such as "edible red things" for Team 2. Assign each of the remaining teams a different category.

Instruct each team to secretly brainstorm *as many as* 10 items that fit its category. Teams will want to list unusual or creative ideas to try to stump the other teams. Allow several minutes for lists to be prepared and then announce that no more additions or changes may be made.

Restate Team 1's category and tell remaining teams that they are to try to guess the items on Team 1's list. Individuals will guess one at a time in the following order: the first player from Team 2 guesses first, followed by the first player from Team 3... the second player from Team 2, the second player from Team 3...

An individual who names an item on Team 1's list earns a point for his own team. Correct or not, play passes to the next guesser. Allow no more than 10 - 15 seconds for a response before moving on. Team 1 crosses from its list all words that are guessed by other teams. Guessing continues until everyone has had one chance to respond. (If teams do not have the same number of members, some teams may have a player guess twice so that all teams have an equal number of scoring opportunities.)

When all guessing is finished award one point to Team 1 for each of the words remaining on its list. If, however, a word on the list does not fit the given category, award *two points* to each of the other teams.

Repeat the procedure by restating Team 2's category and asking for guesses. The first player on Team 3 guesses first, and so on. Continue in this fashion until all lists have been revealed. If time allows, assign each team a new category and begin again. Total all points when finished. The team with the most is the winner.

MODIFICATIONS: In classrooms with a small number of students each person can be his own team and make his own list for other players to guess.

For students who have difficulty writing lists, ask the team to whisper answers to the teacher who will record its responses. Accept the first ten suggestions presented by the team. Then ask other teams to guess what was written before assisting the next team with its list.

❖ ● ♌

Category List

Edible red things
Things that roll
Things you can see through
Things with a lid
Things you cut
Things you can pick
Striped things
Things that roll up
Funny things
Glass things
Christmas things
Things you turn
Reasons to celebrate
Foods eaten with your fingers
Things in a bottle
Famous animals
Things with a handle
Things with doors
Sticky things
Winter things
Words for noises
Bathroom items
Things that come in pairs
Tiny things
Things that light up
Crowded places
Things with zippers
Things that go around
Expensive things
Pizza toppings
Salty things
Things in a newspaper

(See CATEGORY RESOURCE LIST in the appendix for additional suggestions.)

GET THEM BEDDED DOWN

Students will listen to a sentence, and identify an embedded word that fits a specified category.

OBJECTIVES: Vocabulary
Categories
Auditory association & memory
Thinking

TARGET POPULATION: Grades 3 & above
MATERIALS: Chalk & chalkboard
Sentence List (provided)
Tickets (copy one/student from appendix)

PROCEDURE: Give each student a guessing ticket and explain that no answer may be given without it. Collect the ticket of any student who gives a *correct* response. The object is for all students to spend their tickets before there are a total of ten incorrect responses tallied on the chalkboard.

Explain to the class that a category will be announced and a sentence will be read. Within the sentence will be an embedded word that will fit the given category. For example, in the sentence, "It's not nice to yell, Otis", all students who can hear a color word will raise their tickets and prepare to answer, "yellow". Students should not raise their hands until the entire sentence has been read. Select a student to answer, and collect his ticket, if he is correct. Then state the next category, and slowly read the corresponding sentence. Do not emphasize the embedded word. Again select a student with a ticket to respond.

If a student answers incorrectly, put a tally mark on the chalkboard, and choose another student to attempt the same sentence. Do not collect the ticket of the incorrect respondent, who is not allowed to guess again for this sentence. Select only those students who want to respond as indicated by their raised hands. If no student wishes to guess, put a tally mark on the chalkboard and reveal the answer. Also add a tally mark to the board any time an answer is heard from a student who has not been asked to respond.

Continue the procedure until all students have spent their tickets, or until the designated ten tally marks have been reached. If time allows, redistribute tickets and play again.

MODIFICATIONS:

GET THEM BEDDED DOWN

Sentence List

Instrument - Pick a low number to fill in the blank.	(piccolo)
Tool - We should try to help liars stop lying.	(pliers)
State - I owe a dollar for her flowers.	(Iowa)
Vehicle - They ran out of air, plain and simple.	(airplane)
Sport - Bubba said he's going to sock her in the nose.	(soccer)
Vegetable - Are you sick or not?	(corn)
Clothing - It takes oxygen for us to live.	(socks)
Fruit - I will help each of you in a moment.	(peach)
Furniture - Miguel bought some good Eskimo pies.	(desk)
Doll - Will everything on the potato bar be hot?	(Barbie)
Building - Alice tore her blouse on a nail.	(store)
Animal - My father would never cheat a child.	(cheetah)
Appliance - I earn money by shoveling snow.	(iron)
Body part - Sheena just wants a sliver of pie.	(liver)
Flower - For days Eli would not get out of bed.	(daisy)
Beverage - Did you understand the pun, Chuck?	(punch)
Tree - She didn't know her dog would follow her.	(dogwood)
Insect - Clay debugged his apartment yesterday.	(ladybug)
Shape - May I ask where you were yesterday?	(square)
Month - Did Omar change his mind about going?	(March)
Country - There is less pain if I stay off my foot.	(Spain)
Bird - I saw Rob in the general store yesterday.	(robin)
Number - I hope you get well, Valerie.	(twelve)
Bug - I spied her walking along the tracks.	(spider)
Feeling - Wendy pressed the wrong button.	(depressed)
Color - It's not nice to yell, Otis.	(yellow)
Number - You must both read that story.	(three)
Candy - There's an "m" in Emily's middle name, too.	(m & m)
Meat - I want to bake another cake.	(bacon)
Jewelry - Frank let the cat out of the basement.	(anklet)
Medicine - We selected a class princess today.	(aspirin)
Room - Stealing second base meant a near victory.	(basement)
Music style - They walked down the bridge as instructed.	(jazz)
Clothing - Florida is wetter than New Mexico.	(sweater)
Building - The teacher chose the date for the dance.	(church)
Furniture - Ani tried to dress her pup in baby clothes.	(dresser)

THE RIGHT START

Teams will list as many items as possible that fit a stated category, earning extra points for items that begin with a given sound.

OBJECTIVES: Creativity
Categories
Auditory memory & association
Teamwork, Strategies
Vocabulary

TARGET POPULATION: Grades 2 & above
MATERIALS: Paper & pencil/team
Categories List (provided)
Chalk & chalkboard
Clock with second hand (optional)

PROCEDURE: Divide students into teams of 4 or 5, and designate one recorder per team. Give each recorder pencil and paper.

Explain to students that a category will be named and that all teams will be given one minute to record as many items as they can to fit that category. Instruct teams to be creative since points will be earned only for responses that *no other team* records. The exception to this scoring rule is that each team will receive two points for each written word that fits the category and begins with the designated sound, regardless of whether other teams have chosen the same answer. Stress that to receive bonus points an answer must start with a given *sound*, not necessarily a given letter. For example, if the category is "shapes", and the given sound is "s", two points would be awarded to each team for recording each of the following: "circle", "star", "square", and "semicircle".

Announce a category and a bonus sound and begin timing. At the end of one minute announce that no more recording may be done. Begin with any team and ask its recorder to state his first response, and then his second... until all of his answers have been revealed. Any time that a response earns two bonus points award the points to all teams who have recorded it, and then have them cross the word from their lists. If a response is appropriate, but doesn't qualify for bonus points, ask if any other team has written the same response. If so, no team earns points for it, and recorders must cross that word from their lists. If a response is inappropriate, the team must also cross off that word. Ask the next team for the items still remaining on its list. Again have all teams cross off duplicated words.

After all responses have been revealed have each recorder count the number of words that remain on his list. Award one point for each.

Repeat the procedure by choosing another category and stating the beginning sound that will earn bonus points. Continue as long as time allows. Then total all points and declare the team with the most to be the winner.

MODIFICATIONS: Accept only answers that begin with the bonus sound.

Categories List

Categories	Bonus Starting Sounds	Examples for Bonus Points
animal	F	fish, frog, ferret, pheasant, fly, flea
clothing	SH	shirt, shawl, shoe, shorts
colors	P	pink, purple, plum, peach, periwinkle
shapes	S	square, circle, star, semicircle, sphere
fruit	P	plum, prune, peach, pear, pineapple
vegetables	K	carrot, cucumber, cauliflower, corn, cabbage, kale
vehicles	B	bus, bike, Buick, bulldozer, boat, Bronco
beverages	K	coffee, cola, Kool-Aid, cranberry juice, cocoa
furniture	B	bed, bookcase, buffet, bench, barstool
girls' names	D	Denise, Dorothy, Danielle, Donna, Daisy
boys' names	J	James, Julius, Jesse, Joseph, Justin
school subjects	S	social studies, science, spelling, psychology
U.S. states	M	Minnesota, Maine, Montana, Maryland, Michigan
footwear	S	sandals, sneakers, socks, stockings
body parts	L	liver, lungs, legs, lips, lap
sports	B	baseball, bowling, basketball, bicycling
feelings	F	frustrated, foolish, frightened, fearful, fearless
bodies of water	P	pool, pond, puddle, Pacific Ocean
communication	T	talking, telephone, telegraph, TTY
beach things	W	water wings, water, waves, whales
occupations	D	ditch digger, dentist, doctor, doorman
weather words	C	climate, cloudy, cold, cool, clear
insects	M	moth, mosquito, mantis, mite
spices	S	salt, cinnamon, sage, celery seed
meats	H	hot dog, hamburger, ham
plants	R	rose, rhododendron, radish, raspberry bush
transportation	S	scooter, cycle, skis, school bus, submarine
body parts	H	heart, hands, head, heels, hips, hair
parts of a house	B	basement, bedroom, bathroom, bricks, beams
toys	T	truck, top, trampoline, tire swing, teeter-totter

TIC CAT TOE

Students will name four items that fit the category named in a square of at tic tac toe grid.

OBJECTIVES: Vocabulary
Categories
Strategies

TARGET POPULATION: Grades 1 & above
MATERIALS: Chalkboard and chalk
Category List (provided)

PROCEDURE: Divide the class into two groups, Team "X" and Team "O". On the chalkboard draw a 3 x 3 tic tac toe grid. Label each of the nine boxes of the grid with a category such as "zoo animals" from the provided list.

The first person from Team X comes to the board and chooses the place where she would like to place her team's mark. She reads aloud the label in that box, and then names four items that suit that category. If all of her words fit the category, she enters her team's mark in the selected space. Play then passes to the other team. If any or all of the student's responses are incorrect, she receives no mark for her team, and play still passes to the opponent. Be sure that every team member has the opportunity to respond once before anyone gets a second turn.

The first team to get three marks in a row horizontally, vertically , or diagonally wins the game. Begin again, if desired.

MODIFICATIONS: A 4 x 4 grid could be used to extend the game board. The first team to get four marks in a row *or* a mark in each corner wins.

Choose categories that relate to your curriculum to use this game as a review. For example, when reviewing a unit on weather, categories could include "types of clouds", "types of precipitation", "destructive weather", etc.

Allow teams to steal a square previously won by the opponent by naming four *additional* items that fit the category.

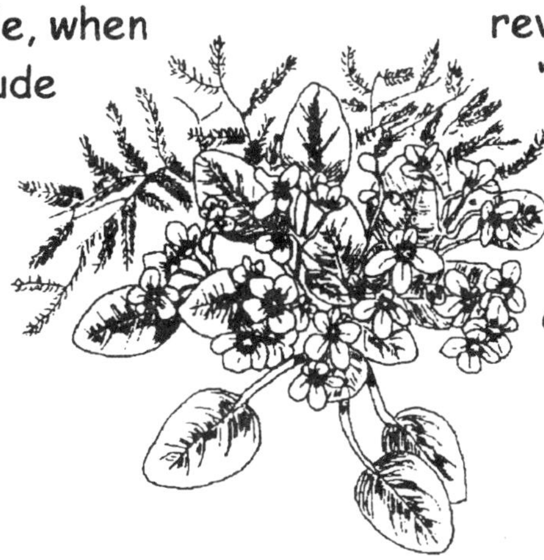

Category Suggestions for Lower Levels

zoo animals
farm animals
body parts
trees
holidays
tools
kinds of cookies
seasons
school subjects
beverages
sports
school things

cartoon characters
teachers' names
toys
birds
relatives
things in the sky
road signs
shapes
2-syllable words
junk food
liquids
sports

baby animals
girls' names
furniture
flowers
types of stores
bugs
camping gear
vegetables
kinds of pie
playground equipment
things that smell good
musical instruments

Category Suggestions for Upper Levels

occupations
non-green vegetables
winter clothing
illegal activities
breakable things
cold things
planets
foreign languages
presidents of the US
state capitols
movie stars
circus acts
military ranks

naturally white things
things that smell bad
things made of paper
countries
footwear
authors' names
salty things
things that sting
Olympic events
gemstones
types of cars
snakes
animal sounds

normally wet things
things that use batteries
things to do while sitting
things that go on walls
things that can be poured
winter activities
things that have corners
types of fabric
types of animal homes
mountain ranges
numbers divisible by 9
pro sports teams
people in uniforms

(See CATEGORY RESOURCE LIST in the appendix for additional suggestions.)

SECRET WORD

Students will try to guess a secret word from given clues.

OBJECTIVES: Vocabulary, Thinking
Auditory association & memory
Teamwork, Categories

TARGET POPULATION: Grades 2 - 5
MATERIALS: Clue List (provided)
Chalkboard & chalk

PROCEDURE: Divide students into several teams and designate one person from each team to be "It". Explain that after hearing a clue, the person who is It will try to guess a secret word without assistance from teammates. If he successfully does so after only one clue, he earns five points for his team. If he is incorrect, the second clue is given to the same spokesperson. If he is now correct, he earns four points for his team. Each time he is incorrect, the next clue is given. With each additional clue, the possible number of points to be earned is reduced by one. A secret word guessed on the fifth clue, therefore, earns only one point. After a spokesperson has given one guess for each of his first three clues, he may ask his teammates to suggest responses for the final two clues.

Begin with Team 1's spokesperson. Give him the first clue that is written below the secret word on the provided clue list. The first clue always tells the category that the word fits. Continue giving clues until the correct answer is revealed. If a team does not identify the secret word, ask for volunteers from the class to do so but award no points.

Tally on the chalkboard the points earned by Team 1. Repeat the procedure with Team 2 by giving clues for another secret word. When each team has had one turn, assign a new person from each team to be It and proceed as described. Continue the activity until each person has been It at least once. Be certain that each team has an equal number of turns to respond, even if some teams must have someone respond twice.

Total all scores when finished. The team with the most points is the winner.

MODIFICATIONS: ❖ ⌨ ❄ ⚐ ♌ ✌

Clue List

POINTS:	GRAPES	KANGAROO	CARROT	HELICOPTER	DIAMOND
5	fruit	animal	vegetable	vehicle	gemstone
4	round	hopping	crunchy	military	expensive
3	small	Australian	long	noisy	hard
2	juicy	short-armed	slender	rotary	faceted
1	green	pouched	orange	hovering	sparkly
	FLOWER	JEANS	TORNADO	MOUSE	G. WASHINGTON
	delicate	clothing	weather	animal	American
	living	pocketed	sudden	tiny	historical
	colorful	heavy	windy	quick	white-haired
	fragrant	blue	destructive	quiet	military
	cultivated	denim	twisting	cheese-eating	presidential
	BOAT	SUITCASE	POPSICLE	COMPUTER	CIRCUS
	vehicle	container	snack	machine	entertainment
	motorized	lockable	sweet	expensive	fast-paced
	topless	rectangular	flavored	high-tech	tented
	waterproof	handled	cold	bootable	colorful
	floating	traveling	frozen	programmed	3-ringed
	SALT	CHILI	HEART	TRAMPOLINE	WRISTWATCH
	mineral	food	body part	plaything	jewelry
	white	hot	internal	round	practical
	granular	Mexican	fist-sized	outdoor	buckled
	flavorful	spicy	bloody	dangerous	numbered
	sprinkled	soupy	pumping	bouncy	ticking
	DINOSAUR	ASTRONAUT	ROOF	COOKIE	FLASHLIGHT
	Animal	occupation	house part	dessert	equipment
	large	high-tech	protective	sweet	hand-held
	varied	scientific	slanted	crunchy	lightweight
	pre-historic	flying	exterior	round	battery operated
	extinct	moon-bound	shingled	chocolate-chip	illuminating

CLASSIFICATION CREATION

Students will classify their own given words with words given to others.

OBJECTIVES: Classification
Vocabulary, Teamwork
Thinking, Creativity

TARGET POPULATION: Grades 2 & above
MATERIALS: Word Cards (copy)
Chalkboard & chalk
Tape

PROCEDURE: Shuffle the deck of provided word cards and deal one card to each student. After reading his card each student tapes it to his shirt, his forehead, or somewhere else that is easily visible. Instruct all students to roam the room in search of others who have cards which can be combined with their own to form a category as described below. When a pair of students thinks that a category can be formed from their word combinations, the two lock arms and raise their free hands. When several pairs are ready to respond say, "Freeze". All students must silently stop in their tracks and listen.

Select one pair and separately point to each member, so that he can announce the word on his card. Then ask the pair to state its category. If correct, write the category and the pair of words on the chalkboard. Then ask if anyone else has a word that could also fit into that category. Write those words on the chalkboard as well. Repeat this procedure with all other pairs who are ready to respond. When all have finished say, "Resume", and all students, including those who have already responded, continue to search for partners to create *new* categories.

Categories can be formed in any way that the two words on students' cards are similar. Acceptable categories might include: vehicles, round things, words that start with "m", red things, words with two syllables, expensive things, words with five letters...

When students can find no more partners, or when a sufficient amount of time has elapsed, ask one student to come to the chalkboard to point out each category that his word fits. This allows students to see that words can be classified in a variety of ways. When this student has finished, challenge classmates to find additional categories from the board that the student may have missed. Write his words under all appropriate categories.

Call the next student to the chalkboard to point out the categories for his word, and repeat the above process. Conclude the activity when all have finished this task.

MODIFICATIONS: This activity could be played for points by dividing students into two teams. Team members could be distinguished by symbols drawn on each of the word cards. For example, draw stars on the cards of one team, and moons on the other. Each time a legitimate partnership is created for a category, award one point to the team of each of the partners. The partnership, therefore, could consist of two people from one team (two points for that team), or one from each team (one point for each). When time expires total the points to see which team has earned the most.

Following one of the procedures above, do not allow partnerships to be formed unless three or more students join forces.

In order to challenge students, periodically announce categories that will no longer be acceptable. For example, when "5-letter words" has been used, announce that no new pairs may be based on the number of letters.

Word Cards

umbrella	sweeper	triangle
nickel	eagle	balloons

flashlight	shirt	wagon
roof	scarf	vest
computer	basement	baseball
bubbles	scissors	necklace
van	chipmunk	shampoo

cherry	knife	chili
radio	pelican	tricycle
pickles	toaster	dollar
horse	cheese	ice cube
horn	chair	ring

PERFECT FIT

Students will write words for a given category when given the first and last letters of the response.

OBJECTIVES: Vocabulary, Strategies
Classification, Teamwork
Creativity, Thinking

TARGET POPULATION: Grades 3 & above
MATERIALS: Perfect Fit Grid (copy one/team)
Chalkboard & chalk, Pencil/team
Perfect Fit Puzzles (provided)

PROCEDURE: Divide students into teams. Select a recorder for each and give him a pencil and a blank Perfect Fit Grid. Based on the ability level of the class, select one of the provided grids and draw it on the chalkboard. Do *not* write the response examples listed in parentheses. Notice that the beginning letter of each word is the ending letter of the preceding word.

Have recorders fill in their grids to match the one on the board. Allow teammates to work together to record as many responses as possible for all positions on the grid. A correct response is one that fits the category listed above it and begins and ends with the given letters. Inform teams of how points are earned as described below.

After a sufficient amount of time announce, "Pencils down". Go to the first answer space on the grid and ask each recorder to tell what response(s) his team has written. Award two points for each correct response in all categories but the last. Award one point for each correct response in the final category, since no final letter is given for that column. For example, using the first puzzle below, Team 1 would receive four points for writing "clasp" and "cap" under "things to wear". Team 2 would receive two points for "cap", and so on. Tally each team's points and move to the next category to the right. On the same grid the next category is "a fruit that begins with 'p' and ends with 'e' ". Tally points for correct responses and check all other categories on the top line of the grid.

After hearing all responses for the entire top line, award four bonus points to each team that had at least one correct response in every position across the line (something to wear, a fruit, a tree, and an insect). Award three bonus points to any team who correctly filled three of the four spaces.

Continue scoring the second line of responses as above, including bonus points for each line, until all points have been awarded for the entire grid. The team with the most points at the end of the activity wins.

MODIFICATIONS: ✍ ♒ ♌ ❖ ⚐ ⌘ ⚑ ✋

Perfect Fit Puzzles

(Do not copy this section for students. One possible answer is written in parentheses.)

1.

	THINGS TO WEAR		FRUITS		TREES		INSECTS
C	(cap)	P	(prune)	E	(elm)	M	(moth)
B	(belt)	T	(tomato)	O	(oak)	K	(katydid)
W	(watch)	H	(honeydew)	W	(willow)	W	(wasp)

2.

	ADJECTIVES		NOUNS		VERBS		ADVERBS
T	(tame)	E	(ear)	R	(roar)	R	(rarely)
S	(sweet)	T	(tent)	T	(tell)	L	(luckily)
C	(clever)	R	(road)	D	(drag)	G	(gladly)

3.

	FOODS		COLORS		ANIMALS		VEHICLES
P	(peas)	S	(silver)	R	(rabbit)	T	(truck)
P	(potato)	O	(orange)	E	(eel)	L	**(limousine)**
H	(hot dog)	G	(gold)	D	(dinosaur)	R	(rocket)

4.

	FRUITS		SPORTS		COLORS		STATES
P	(peach)	H	(hockey)	Y	(yellow)	W	(Wyoming)
P	(pear)	R	(rowing)	G	(green)	N	(New Jersey)
K	(kiwi)	I	(ice skating)	G	(gold)	D	(Delaware)

5.

	BODY PARTS		COLORS		ANIMALS		CAREERS
H	(hair)	R	(red)	D	(dog)	G	(gardener)
E	(elbow)	W	(white)	E	(eagle)	E	(engineer)
L	(lip)	P	(pink)	K	(kangaroo)	O	(operator)

-----------------(Put category headings at the top of each column. Put beginning & ending letters on short lines.)-----------------

Perfect Fit Grid

___ ___	___ ___	___ ___	___
___ ___	___ ___	___ ___	___
___ ___	___ ___	___ ___	___

CRISS-CROSS CATEGORIES

Students will link together in crossword fashion several words that fit a given category.

OBJECTIVES: Vocabulary, Categories
Teamwork, Strategies
Thinking

TARGET POPULATION: Grades 2 & above
MATERIALS: Chalkboard & chalk
Category List (provided)

PROCEDURE: Divide the class into 4 or 5 teams. Within each team select two people to be partners for the first round.

State a category from the provided list. Have *one* of the partners from each team come to the board, and allow her 15 seconds to print a word that fits the stated category. Help students with spelling, if necessary. Each player's partner then comes to the board. She has 30 seconds to attach to her teammate's word another word that fits the category. She does this by using one of the letters from the previously written word, as in a crossword puzzle. For example, if the category is "fruit" and the first player writes "A P P L E", her partner could then write "L E M O N" as follows:

```
        L          A
    APPLE          P
        M    or    P
        O          LEMON
        N          E
```

If both words fit the category, award two points. Award one point if only one of the words fits or if only one word is written.

No players at the board are allowed to write the same word. The first person to finish writing a particular word gets to keep it. Partners may not confer or receive help from other teammates.

Record points on the chalkboard. Erase the criss-cross words and announce a new category for the next set of partners from each team. Follow the same procedure for as long as time allows and then total all points. The team with the most points wins.

MODIFICATIONS: To make this activity more challenging, allow upper level students to attempt to link three, four, or more words in the same fashion. Award extra points for longer chains of words.

Allow the second player of each pair to link as many related words as she can within her given 30 seconds.

In upper grades the first person could print a word that fits the category with her partners crossing it with adjectives that describe it. In the category of "fruit" the following is such an example:

```
       ROUND
   APPLE      J
       DELICIOUS
              I
              C
              Y
```

Category List

occupations
creatures with shells
kinds of fish
things you pull
things you do with your hands
things you do with your feet
states
countries
cities
things in a parade
liquids
baby animals
measuring items
things you wear on your head
words that start with "p"
things you turn on
forest things
parts of a pizza
indoor games
parts of the body
musical instruments
storybook characters
desserts
holidays
pets
transportation
cereals
drinks
kitchen items
things that need batteries
vegetables
noisy things
Halloween costumes
parts of a car
school subjects
sports

CAT BINGO

Students will determine if a given sentence contains words that fit the categories on their bingo grids.

OBJECTIVES: Vocabulary
Classification
Auditory association & memory

TARGET POPULATION: Grades 3 - 7
MATERIALS: Bingo Grids (copy one/student)
Classification Sentence List (provided)
Pencil/student

PROCEDURE: Give each student a copy of the bingo grid which includes a list of thirty categories. Instruct all students to complete their grids by writing a different category from the list in each of the sixteen squares. They may choose any categories they want and write them in any order. Each bingo card prepared in this way will be unique.

When students have prepared their cards, instruct them to listen carefully to the sentence that will be read. They are to listen for the two items in the sentence that will fit the listed categories. If either or both of the words of the sentence fit categories that were written on a student's grid, she is to mark an X in the square where the category appears.

Slowly repeat the sentence once or twice to give everyone a chance to discover the category words. (Note: Emphasizing the targeted words as you read the sentence will aid students who have difficulty with auditory association skills.) Keep track of the sentences that were read to make it easier to verify winning bingo cards.

The game proceeds as above with additional sentences from the provided list. The first student to mark four category squares in a row horizontally, vertically, or diagonally calls, "Bingo". Have the potential winner name the four categories that she has marked. Check to make sure that these categories were indeed in the given sentences. To get credit for the win, however, the student must also name another word that would fit in each of those four categories. Continue playing until three or four students have achieved "Bingo". Winners should continue to try for a second win.

MODIFICATIONS: The game can be played with two players sharing bingo cards. This will help students who have difficulty functioning independently.

Play a second time with the same bingo grid by making up new sentences and having students use a different writing instrument to mark the squares.

Instead of using the provided sentences, read only the category words for students to classify.

To challenge upper level students see the CATEGORY RESOURCE LIST in the appendix.

❄ ⌘

Sentence List

I studied my *spelling* while I ate some *pudding.* (subjects, desserts)
The *cardinal* flew into the *dogwood.* (birds, trees)
In *January* he broke his *ankle.* (body parts)
My *uncle* loves to listen to *gospel songs.* (relatives, music)
The *grasshopper* crawled on the *purple* flowers. (bugs, colors)
That bratty kid spilled *milk* all over my *newspaper.* (liquid, things to read)
Apartments are very expensive in *Chicago.* (buildings, cities)
I left my *raincoat* beside the *refrigerator.* (clothing, kitchen things)
That young *poodle* jumped onto the *sofa.* (dogs, furniture)
Roddy needs a better *screwdriver.* (boys' names, tools)
On *Thursday* he bought a new *Jeep.* (days of week, vehicles)
The *cashier* ripped the *linen.* (jobs, fabric)
The *yo-yo* had shiny *stars* all over it. (toys, shapes)
Over *Thanksgiving* break we're going to a *hockey* game. (holidays, sports)
She dropped her *banana* on a picture of *Saturn.* (fruits, planets)

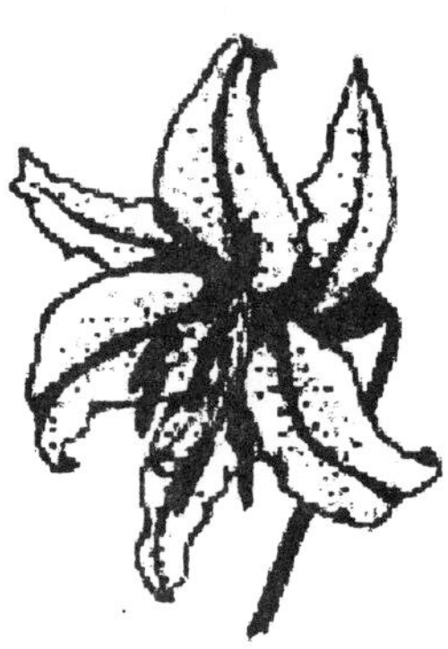 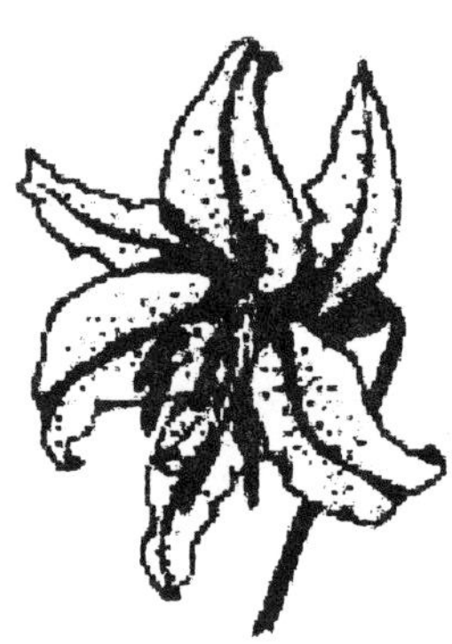 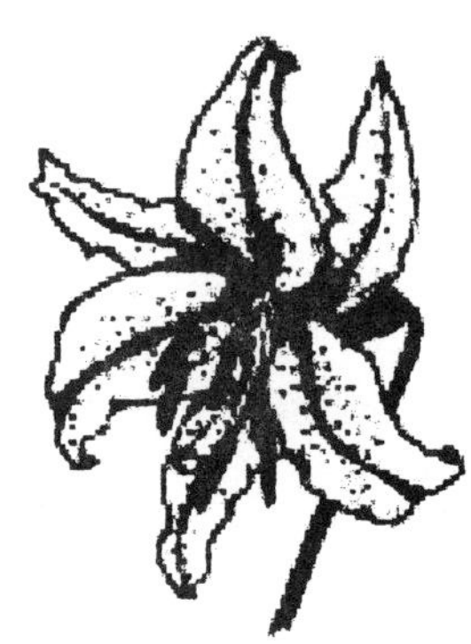

Cat Bingo Grid

Category Word Bank

dogs	fruits	boys' names	furniture	buildings
body parts	trees	holidays	things to read	clothing
jobs	liquids	shapes	months	planets
bugs	birds	colors	fabric	days of the week
toys	vehicles	kitchen things	relatives	desserts
cities	tools	school subjects	sports	kinds of music

CLASS-Y BINGO

Students will listen to a list of related words and identify the category.

OBJECTIVES: Vocabulary
Classification, Thinking
Auditory association & memory

TARGET POPULATION: Grades 2 & above
MATERIALS: Category List (provided)
Class-y Bingo Grids (copy one/student)
Pencil/student

PROCEDURE: Give each student a copy of the Class-y Bingo Grid, which includes a list of 25 categories. Tell students to complete their grids by writing one category from the list in each of the sixteen squares, but not in the order given. Each bingo card prepared in this manner will be unique.

When students have completed their grids instruct them to listen to the four words that will be read. Students must identify the category that the given list fits and, if that category is written on their grids, mark an X in the appropriate square. Do *not* announce the category at this time. Slowly repeat the list several times. Keep track of the categories that have been read to make it easier to verify winning bingo cards.

The game proceeds as above with additional category lists being read. The first student to mark four squares in a row vertically, horizontally, or diagonally calls, "Bingo". Have the potential winner name the four categories that she has marked, and check to make sure that they were indeed called. To get credit for the win the student must name <u>another</u> (unread) word that would fit each of those categories.

Continue playing until several students have achieved "Bingo". Students who have already won should continue to try for a second win.

To use the same bingo cards to play again, have students use a crayon or marker for the next game.

MODIFICATIONS: The game could be played in pairs with two students sharing bingo grids. This will help students who have difficulty functioning independently.

Category List

(Do not read the NAME of the category, just the items listed.)

BUGS	DOGS	FURNITURE	TREES	4-SYLLABLE WORDS
ant	beagle	recliner	beech	chrysanthemum
wasp	poodle	sofa	palm	unemployment
mosquito	shepherd	table	spruce	Mississippi
honey bee	retriever	stand	sycamore	communicate

DRINKS	TOOLS	MACHINES	HOLIDAYS	SPORTS
milk	hammer	lawn mower	Halloween	volleyball
soda	screwdriver	vacuum cleaner	4th of July	soccer
juice	drill	water pump	Thanksgiving	golf
tea	saw	air conditioner	President's Day	tennis

CLOTHING	VEGETABLES	BODY PARTS	GEMSTONES	HOMES
shirt	onion	chest	diamond	nest
dress	celery	thigh	emerald	burrow
sock	broccoli	neck	amethyst	apartment
coat	lettuce	shoulder	ruby	den

BABY ANIMALS	BODIES OF WATER	MUSICAL INSTRUMENTS	WOODEN THINGS	PIZZA TOPPINGS
kitten	lake	accordion	table	green peppers
cub	ocean	trombone	baseball bat	cheese
calf	puddle	banjo	house	pepperoni
fawn	river	xylophone	guitar	olives

THINGS THAT FLY	WHITE FOODS	SCHOOL SUBJECTS	HOT THINGS	SPICES/ HERBS
bird	milk	math	sun	oregano
kite	cream cheese	English	fire	cinnamon
airplane	potatoes	social studies	summertime	dill
helicopter	sugar	spelling	steam	garlic

Class-y Bingo Grid

Categories List

baby animals	white foods	gemstones	wooden things	musical instruments
bodies of water	bugs	vegetables	body parts	clothing
homes	sports	dogs	furniture	school subjects
trees	drinks	tools	machines	4-syllable words
holidays	spices/herbs	hot things	pizza toppings	things that fly

TERM ME ON

Students will identify the term that fits a pair of given words.

OBJECTIVES: Vocabulary, Auditory association
Antonyms, Synonyms, Thinking
Compounds, Contractions
Homophones, Palindromes
Possessives, Plurals, Strategies
Prefixes, Suffixes, Base words

TARGET POPULATION: Grades 3 & above
MATERIALS: Chalkboard & chalk
Word Pair List (provided)

PROCEDURE: Divide the class into Team A, Team B, and Team C. Write one of the following two lists on the board, depending on the vocabulary cluster chosen for review.

List 1	List 2
COMPOUND WORDS	PALINDROMES
POSSESSIVES	ANTONYMS
PREFIXES	SYNONYMS
SUFFIXES	HOMOPHONES
CONTRACTIONS	PLURALS

Select one student from each team to be the team "expert" and have all experts come to the front of the room. On the chalkboard draw and label the following grid:

A1	B1	C1
A2	B2	C2
A3	B3	C3

Teams will attempt to respond correctly in order to be the first to earn three marks in a row horizontally, vertically, or diagonally.

Have the first player from Team A (not the expert) stand. Ask him to state the square that he hopes to fill with his team's mark. Teammates may not assist with this selection nor with the player's response.

If the standing player selects "B3", for example, the expert from Team B will actually be the one to state the answer. His choices for responses are the words listed on the chalkboard. Team B's expert gives his response, and then it is up to the standing player to say, "I agree" or "I disagree." If the standing player is correct, his team's mark is placed in square "B3". Incorrect responses earn no marks.

Have the first player from Team B stand and choose a square. This player may select any square except the last one marked. In the above example he may choose any square except "B3", which was just won by Team A. Read another word pair. Again the expert from the chosen column responds and the first player from Team B agrees or disagrees. (NOTE: Experts, if they wish, may intentionally give wrong answers.)

Any time that a player chooses a square for which the expert from his own team must respond, and the standing player correctly agrees or disagrees with that response, the standing player becomes the team's new expert. The previous expert returns to his team.

When it is Team C's turn to respond, the first player may select any square of the grid except the last one marked. This means that he may attempt to win a square that is already occupied by another mark, as long as it was not the last one to be earned.

Continue the activity with the second player from Team A and then each of the other teams. Proceed as described until any team places three of its marks in a row. Begin again, if time allows.

MODIFICATIONS: For upper level students write both lists on the board and provide word pairs from each.

LIST 1

COMP (compound words)	POS (possessives)	PRE (bases + prefixes)	SUF (bases + suffixes)	CON (contractions)

quietly, largest SUF
Mary's, hers POS
bathrobe, into COMP
happily, beautiful SUF
eating, helper SUF
without, goldfish COMP
swatted, teacher SUF
its, Tracey's POS
hasn't, that's CON
bewitch, rename PRE
theirs, Showna's POS

wouldn't, they're CON
submarine, nonsense PRE
slowly, bravest SUF
unlike, misbehave PRE
mother's, Dave's POS
didn't, she'd CON
breakfast, whenever COMP
pretest, disagree PRE
lightly, thankful SUF
we'll, you're CON
disappoint, imperfect PRE

rewrite, precook PRE
outside, nowhere COMP
misuse, semicircle PRE
I'll, won't CON
baseball, takeout COMP
undress, defrost PRE
mine, yours POS
can't, he's CON
birdbath, anyone COMP
employee, audible SUF
peanut, something COMP

LIST 2

PAL (palindromes)	ANT (antonyms)	SYN (synonyms)	HOM (homophones)	PLU (plurals)

strong, weak ANT
deed, pop PAL
noon, redder PAL
tired, sleepy SYN
refuse, accept ANT
connect, join SYN
toss, catch ANT
writer, author SYN
pup, level PAL
smile, grin SYN
children, chairs PLU

empty, vacant SYN
hall, haul HOM
oceans, feet PLU
bury, berry HOM
toot, eve PAL
common, rare ANT
Anna, madam PAL
colonel, kernel HOM
people, sandals PLU
hidden, exposed ANT
chews, choose HOM

peep, sees PAL
poll, pole HOM
dogs, oxen PLU
delicious, tasty SYN
aisle, I'll HOM
never, always ANT
mice, geese PLU
dad, radar PAL
sick, ill SYN
spiders, deer PLU
radios, cars PLU

HEARSAY DETECTIVE

Students will write one compound word from a heavily loaded sentence.

OBJECTIVES: Compounds, Thinking
Vocabulary, Strategies
Auditory memory & association

TARGET POPULATION: Grades 2 & above
MATERIALS: Sentence List (provided)
Paper & pencil/student
Chalkboard & chalk

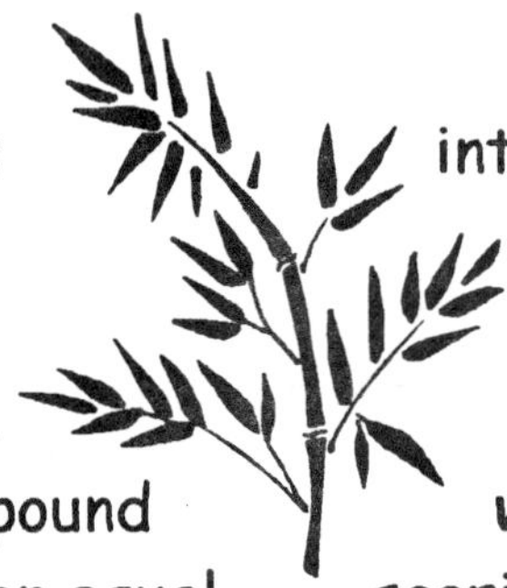

PROCEDURE: Divide the class into teams and provide each student with paper and pencil. If teams cannot be divided evenly, it will be necessary to declare someone from each of the "shorted" teams to be the "double respondent". The double respondent will write two compound words for each sentence. This ensures that all teams are given equal scoring opportunities. Teammates could take turns being the double respondent. Students will be working independently but scoring points for their teams.

Tell students that each of them will be writing down one, *and only one,* compound word from the sentence that will be read. Explain that team points will be kept, and that points will be earned as follows: If a student writes a compound word from the given sentence, *and no more than three students from the class* have chosen that same word, each of the students who has written that compound scores one point for his team. It is possible, therefore, that all of the points may go to the same team. Explain to students that it is to their advantage to choose a compound word that they think few others will select. Copying a word that someone else has written will decrease the chances of earning points.

Read a sentence from the provided list three times so that no one must ask for repetition. When all students are ready with one written response begin checking. This time slowly read the sentence with a pause between each word. When the student hears the teacher say the compound word that he has written, he must immediately raise his hand or be left out of the count. Tally each point as it is earned. Be sure to inform students which words are compounds in the sentence even if no one has selected a particular one.

Continue by reading another sentence three times and following the same procedure. When time expires the team with the most points wins.

MODIFICATIONS: Deduct a point from a team if one of its members writes a word that is not a compound word in the given sentence.

For smaller classes, award a point to the player or team if *no one else* writes the same compound word. Possibly allow each student to choose two compound words for each sentence.

Sentence List

Her classmates used ballpoint pens to underline their homework grades in their notebooks.

The kickoff led to a touchdown; however, the Dallas Cowboys finally won without difficulty.

Your yearbook is inside the classroom in the bookcase near the raincoats.

This Thanksgiving we airmailed some packages overseas to the victims of the earthquakes and the landslides.

Did you hear anything about a motorcyclist who destroyed our mailbox with a crowbar?

This afternoon Allison's boyfriend gave her a birthday cupcake with pineapple frosting.

Santa went downstairs beside the fireplace to get some eggnog and gingerbread.

The homemade earache medicine that her grandfather gave me tasted like grapefruit juice.

When the fireworks began the barefoot kids were eating popcorn on the seesaw at the playground.

Mr. Hillman said that the freshmen were not allowed to play basketball, horseshoes, or leapfrog anymore.

The linebacker and the fullback from that football team were on the sidelines getting their mouthpieces.

Grandmother sent me to the supermarket to get a watermelon and the ingredients to make strawberry milkshakes.

The flowerpots containing snapdragons and rosebuds were full of ladybugs and butterflies.

After the rainstorm the ocean washed many starfish, seashells and dead jellyfish onto the seashore.

The gingerbread and blueberry pancakes that Rosemary had for breakfast gave her heartburn.

The sheet and pillowcase on that waterbed match the wallpaper in my stepmother's bedroom.

The cookbook says that I need applesauce, oatmeal, and cornbread mix to make this meatball recipe.

At bedtime I will put on my nightgown and bathrobe, and then I will hang my party outfit on the bedpost.

The redheaded girl with pigtails is heartbroken because her granddad said she had to get a haircut.

The bulldozer and backhoe operators are working at the sawmill near the junkyard today.

The crazy bricklayer injured his tailbone and his kneecap while he was trying to do handstands and cartwheels.

The footprints of the outlaws were found near the sunporch of the schoolhouse and on Rattlesnake Trail.

My easygoing hairdresser's favorite jukebox song is "Somewhere Over the Rainbow."

Last weekend we went looking around the campground for firewood for the campfire.

Our farmhand made a heavyset scarecrow for the cornfield near the railroad tracks.

JOINT COMPOUND

Students will state a word that can be placed between two given words to form two compound words.

OBJECTIVES: Vocabulary
Compounds
Thinking

TARGET POPULATION: Grades 3 & above
MATERIALS: Compound Word List (provided)
Tickets (copy 2/team from appendix)
Chalkboard & chalk
1 Magnet or self-stick note/team

PROCEDURE: On the chalkboard draw a simple set of stairs with as many steps as desired. Divide the class into 3 - 5 teams and assign each a team number. Label self-stick notes with one team number each, or if possible, use a variety of magnets for markers. Select one person from each team to come to the front of the room. Give each of these students two tickets that may be used to buy guesses. When a student has spent both of his tickets, he may no longer guess.

On the chalkboard write one of the word pairs from the provided list. Be sure to put the same number of dashes between the words, as there are letters in the missing word. Students are to think of a word that could replace the dashes to form one compound word with the word preceding it, and a different compound word with the word following it.

As soon as the word pair is written on the board, ticket holders may raise their hands to guess. If more than one person wants to answer, choose the student whose hand was raised first. Take one of his tickets and ask for his response. If he is correct, count the number of blank dashes between the word pairs on the board. This number will tell how many steps each of the other teams will be penalized. For example, if there are three blank dashes, each of the teams, except the one that guessed correctly, must move its self-stick note (or magnet) up three steps. The goal for each team is to keep as far away from the top step as possible.

If the first guesser is incorrect, or if no one decides to guess, fill in the letter that replaces the LAST dash in the hidden word. Again choose the first player, if any, to raise his hand to respond. When all desired guesses have been made and the word is still not identified, fill in the next to the last letter so that two letters will be visible. Continue revealing additional letters as necessary. When the correct answer has been guessed, move each of the markers, except the one representing the correctly responding team, up the steps the number of remaining dashes.

Select new ticket holders for each team and bring them to the front of the room. Write another word pair on the board and proceed as described. Continue playing until one team topples over the edge, or until time expires. The team that is closest to the bottom step wins.

MODIFICATIONS: When a correct response is revealed have someone describe what the word would mean if it were actually a compound word made by all three of the words, such as "redheadshrinker" or "flashlighthouse".

Word Pair List

EAR - - - - ROLL	(drum)	RED - - - - SHRINKER	(head)
GRAPE - - - - - CAKE	(fruit)	DRAGON - - - SWATTER	(fly)
PICK - - - - - - BOOK	(pocket)	GREEN - - - - - COAT	(house)
PITCH - - - - LIFT	(fork)	SWIM - - - - CASE	(suit)
POP - - - - COB	(corn)	SWEET - - - - - BEAT	(heart)
THUNDER - - - - - BURST	(cloud)	EVERY - - - TIME	(day)
DAY - - - ROOM	(bed)	AIR - - - - - ROPE	(tight)
BOOK - - - - - KEEPER	(store)	OUT - - - - KNOB	(door)
APPLE - - - - - PAN	(sauce)	GRAND - - - - - BIRTH	(child)
COURT - - - - MATE	(room)	PAPER - - - FRIEND	(boy)
SIDE - - - - STAND	(kick)	PULL - - - - TIME	(over)
QUICK - - - - STONE	(sand)	BACK - - - - FLY	(fire)
BIRD - - - - - STORM	(brain)	FIRST - - - - SHAKE	(hand)
HORSE - - - - STRING	(shoe)		
DRY - - - - PAPER	(wall)		
CROW - - - BELL	(bar)		
DISH - - - CAKE	(pan)		
SHORT - - - - LIGHT	(stop)		
FLASH - - - - - HOUSE	(light)		
BULL - - - CATCHER	(dog)		
BLACK - - - - BOX	(mail)		
BARE - - - - BALL	(foot)		
PINK - - - LASH	(eye)		
NOTE - - - - WORM	(book)		
HOME - - - - OUT	(work)		

WRAP-AROUND COMPOUNDS

Students will use the second part of a compound word to begin a new compound word.

OBJECTIVES: Compounds
Vocabulary
Strategies
Teamwork

TARGET POPULATION: Grades 3 & above
MATERIALS: Paper & pencil/team, Chalkboard & chalk
Compound Starter List (provided)
Dictionary/team (optional)

PROCEDURE: Divide the class into teams and designate a recorder for each. Give all recorders pencil and paper and tell them to divide their papers into three columns by drawing two vertical lines. Select a word from the provided compound starter list and use it in a meaningful sentence. Instruct each recorder to write that word on the top line of the first column of his paper. Select a second word, use it in a sentence, and have recorders place that word at the top of the second column. Select a third word for the last column and use it in a sentence.

The task for each team is to use the second part of the given compound word as the beginning of a new compound word. To continue, each team will use the second half of its *new* word to begin a third word, etc... until players are stumped for another compound. Dictionaries may be used, if desired, to encourage longer lists and vocabulary development.

If teams do not overhear each other, lists are likely to be unique. For example, if the starter word is "someday", lists may start out as follows:

Team 1	Team 2	Team 3	Team 4
someday	someday	someday	someday
daybreak	daylight	daytime	daybed
breakfast...	lighthouse...	timeline...	bedroom...

Each team should work on all three columns of words at the same time. After a specified amount of time has elapsed, or when it appears that all teams are stumped announce, "Pencils down".

Ask Team 1 to read its first new compound word from column one. Write it on the board. To get credit for a correct response, *any* team member must in one attempt use the new compound word in a meaningful sentence. Tally one point for Team 1 if it is able to do so. Ask the same team to state the next word, if any, that it developed in column one. Check each response in succession, and write it on the board. Tally each point as it is earned and discontinue scoring for any of the following reasons:

1) A word is revealed that is not a compound word.
2) The new compound word does not begin with the second half of the previous one.
3) The new compound word is not correctly used in a meaningful sentence.
4) The compound word has already been used in a previous round.

Check each of the other team's responses for column one. Award an extra point to each team for each correct compound on its list that was *not* duplicated by another team. Then check columns two and three in the same manner.

Select new recorders, and instruct them to draw three new columns on the backs of their papers. Announce three more starter words and begin again. Teams may not reuse compounds revealed by any team in previous rounds.

Continue the activity for as long as time allows. Then total all scores and declare the team with the most points to be the winner.

MODIFICATIONS: Put a starter word in each square of a tic tac toe grid. Require that a new compound word be made from the starter word in order to earn the square.

Starter List

someday
whoever
sweetheart
without
toothpick
riverside
homework
cowgirl
freeway
cookbook

cottonmouth
countdown
football
campfire
flashlight
pineapple
blockhead
mockingbird
stepmother
fullback

popcorn
driftwood
farmhand
earring
doorstep
jackhammer
buckeye
blackmail
rainwater
crosswalk

HALF-POUND GRIDS

Students will attach a given word to a word on their grids to form a compound word.

OBJECTIVES: Compounds
Vocabulary
Auditory association

TARGET POPULATION: Grades 3 & above
MATERIALS: Half-Pound Grids (copy one/student)
Other-Half List (provided)
Pencil/student

PROCEDURE: Distribute Half-Pound grids with the attached word list to all students. Instruct them to write a different word from the Half-Pound list in each square of the grid. Students' words should be written on the *solid* line within each square. This will allow room for another word to be written on the dotted line either before or after those words selected and written by the students. Words should not be written in the same order as they are listed. Each grid prepared in this manner should be unique.

When all students have completed their grids, read any word from the provided Other-Half list. Tell students that the given word can be combined with at least one word from the Half-Pound list to form a compound word. The word on the grid may be the first or the second half of the compound word. If a student determines that the teacher-read word can form a compound word with one in her grid, she writes the teacher-read word on the appropriate dotted line. For example, if the teacher-read word is "basket", and a student who has written "waste" on her grid recognizes "wastebasket" as a compound word, she writes "basket" *after* the word "waste". "Basket" could also be written *before* the word "ball" to form "basketball". Each student may use the teacher-read word as many times as it combines with words on her grid. Correct responses are not revealed to the class at this point, but make sure that each child understands the task before moving on.

If a student does not think that the teacher-read word combines with one on her grid, she should write that word on the bottom of her paper for future checking. These words could also be written on the board, if desired.

After a sufficient amount of time read another word from the Other-Half list, and instruct students to determine if its mate is on their grids. Continue presenting additional words, and following the same procedure.

The first person to write three compound words in a row horizontally, vertically, or diagonally calls out, "Three in a row!" In order for this player to claim the win, however, she must use each of the newly formed compound words in a meaningful sentence. If she is unable to do so, the game continues. This player must now achieve a new "Three in a row!" to try again for the win. The first player to use her three aligned compound words in meaningful sentences wins.

Continue the same game until several players, even as many as half of the class, have achieved "Three in a row!" Those who have already won should continue to try for a second win.

If time allows, call out each Other-Half word from the list below and ask for volunteers to tell compounds that can be formed by combining them with Half-Pound words.

MODIFICATIONS: The game could be played with pairs of students sharing grids to help those students who have difficulty functioning independently.

Other-Half List
(For teacher to read aloud)

sun	room	pick
pocket	fold	bar
land	horse	ear
bone	four	way
pot	wheel	dust
off	wood	head
out	home	basket
play	stick	birth
side	eye	board
day	hand	dragon

Half-Pound Grid

Half-Pound List

kick	saw	holder	pin	shake	tail
pen	hunter	radish	yard	dream	mark
sick	waste	drum	be	crow	pick
run	tooth	snap	fit	set	lid
slide	ball	fire	teen	blind	key

TWO HEADS ARE BETTER THAN ONE

Students will guess the two parts of a compound word being pantomimed by a pair of classmates.

OBJECTIVES: Vocabulary, Creativity
Teamwork, Strategies
Compounds

TARGET POPULATION: Grades 2 - 6
MATERIALS: Compound Word List (provided)

PROCEDURE: Arrange students into partners. If there is an uneven number of students, the teacher must also play. Secretly tell each pair a compound word and allow them a few minutes to collaborate. When it is a pair's turn, the two must act out (pantomime without sound) the two parts of the given compound word. One partner acts out one of the words as her mate acts out the other. For example, if the secret word is "toadstool", one partner will act like a "toad", while the other tries to convey "stool". Classmates will try to guess the compound word that is being enacted.

When a compound word is revealed, or after enough time has expired, choose another set of partners to pantomime its word(s).

Continue the activity until each student has had at least one opportunity to pantomime. If time allows, assign each student a new partner and a new compound word, and begin again.

MODIFICATIONS: Post a list of compound words from which the targeted words will be taken. Accept a limited number of guesses.

Have students draw pictures of the two parts of their word on the chalkboard. Others can guess the secret compound word.

Word List

HAND + WRITING	HEAD + LIGHT	STAGE + COACH	LIP + STICK	HOUSE + BOAT
CUP + CAKE	LADY + BUG	SHIP + WRECK	MOUTH + WASH	PITCH + FORK
PLAY + GROUND	POP + CORN	RACE + HORSE	RAIN + BOW	SAND + BOX
SHOE + STRING	SMOKE + STACK	SIDE + WALK	COOK + BOOK	STAR + FISH
STAR + LIGHT	SUIT + CASE	SUN + FLOWER	SEA + FOOD	TOOTH + BRUSH
TREE + HOUSE	UP + STAIRS	WAIST + LINE	WALL + PAPER	WATER + FALL
BACK + BONE	BACK + REST	BALL + ROOM	BOARD + WALK	CRY + BABY
BATH + ROOM	BED + ROOM	BELL + BOTTOMS	BIRD + HOUSE	BOOK + WORM
BOX + CAR	BREAK + FAST	CAMP + FIRE	CAR + SICK	DISH + WASHER
LAND + SLIDE	COW + BELL	COW + BOY	STEP + LADDER	FIRE + MAN

COMPOUND FRACTURES

Students will separate a pair of compound words into their individual parts, and combine a part of each to form a new compound.

OBJECTIVES: Compounds, Thinking
Vocabulary, Strategies
Teamwork

TARGET POPULATION: Grades 3 & above
MATERIALS: Chalkboard & chalk
Compound Word List (provided)

PROCEDURE: Divide students into two or three teams. On the chalkboard write a pair of compound words from the provided list. (Do not write the intended response in parentheses.) Explain to the class that each of the compound words on the board can be broken into two separate words. For example, the word "grapefruit" can be separated into "grape" + "fruit", and "cupcake" into "cup" + "cake". The task for each respondent is to take one word from the first separated compound word and one word from the second, and combine them to make a new compound word. The two words may be combined in either order.

In the above example the following eight possibilities exist: "grapecup", "cupgrape", "fruitcup", "cupfruit", "grapecake", "cakegrape", "fruitcake" and "cakefruit". Responding students must determine which of those possibilities is indeed a compound word. "Fruitcake" is correct in this example.

Have the first player from each team stand. Write a pair of compound words from the provided list on the board and say, "Go". Standing students get *one chance each* to respond, but only the first correct response earns a point. Standing players, if they need assistance, may begin saying various combinations of answers to their teammates who may nod to agree or disagree. Teammates may not speak, however. It is ultimately the responsibility of the standing player to choose her one response. The first student to shout out a correct response earns one point for her team. She may then earn an additional point by using the new compound word in a sentence that shows she understands its meaning.

If a standing student shouts out an incorrect response, she may not respond again. If after a fair amount of time no one has given a correct answer, ask for a volunteer to state the new compound word and use it in a sentence. Award no points in this case.

Have the next player from each team stand, and select another pair of compound words from the provided list. Proceed as described above. After everyone has had one turn, mix up the order of students within the teams so that different combinations of standing players are formed.

Continue the activity for as long as time allows. The team with the most points when finished wins.

MODIFICATIONS: For classrooms with a small number of students form two teams only or have each student be her own team.

Compound Word List

houseboat - outdoors	(outhouse)
homesick - sweetheart	(heartsick)
flowerpot - jackhammer	(jackpot)
teabag - pothole	(teapot)
daylight - housekeeper	(lighthouse)
notebook - farmhand	(handbook)
anyway - indoor	(doorway)
hilltop - downstairs	(downhill)
lawsuit - outburst	(outlaw)
tugboat - motorcycle	(motorboat)
outfit - blackboard	(blackout)
drumstick - earmark	(eardrum)
newspaper - butterfly	(flypaper)
backrub - downstream	(rubdown)
haircut - baseball	(hairball)
mushroom - kickball	(ballroom)
grapefruit - cupcake	(fruitcake)
linebacker - blockhead	(headline)
catfish - eggshell	(shellfish)
teaspoon - tablecloth	(tablespoon)
blueprint - footbridge	(footprint)
warlord - inland	(landlord)
toothbrush - pickax	(toothpick)
drawback - fireplace	(backfire)
pigpen - tailgate	(pigtail)
scarecrow - barbell	(crowbar)
kickball - liftoff	(kickoff)
hopscotch - dumbbell	(bellhop)
snowball - wastebasket	(basketball)
oatmeal - popcorn	(cornmeal)
sunfish - bobcat	(catfish)
paperhanger - drywall	(wallpaper)
battleship - yardstick	(shipyard)
grandmother - doorstep	(stepmother)
birthstone - markdown	(birthmark)
overnight - billboard	(overboard)
newspaper - sandbox	(sandpaper)
storeroom - bookcase	(bookstore)
bedroom - waterfall	(waterbed)
widespread - bedrock	(bedspread)
townhouse - touchdown	(downtown)
campground - horseplay	(playground)
underwear - handstand	(understand)
eyedropper - deadline	(deadeye)

COMPOUND IT!

Students will combine two words from a given sentence to form a compound word.

OBJECTIVES: Vocabulary, Compounds
Auditory memory & association
Thinking, Sentences

TARGET POPULATION: Grades 3 & above
MATERIALS: Chalkboard & chalk
Tickets (copy 2/team from appendix)
Compound Word Sentence List (provided)

PROCEDURE: Divide the class into three teams. Select one member of each team to come to the front of the room, and give each of them two tickets which will be used to buy guesses. When both of a respondent's tickets are spent, she may make no more guesses. Seated classmates may not assist.

Read a sentence from the provided list, or write it on the chalkboard if the task seems too difficult. Inform the three respondents that they are to find two words in the sentence that can be combined to form a compound word. For example, in the sentence "I threw my ball to second base", the words "ball" and "base" can be combined to form "baseball". When a respondent thinks that she knows the intended compound word, she quickly raises her hand. Mentally keep track of the order of hand raising. The first hand-raiser gives the teacher one of her tickets and immediately gives her response. If she is incorrect or fails to answer immediately, select the second person to have raised her hand. Collect her ticket and evaluate her response. The second hand-raiser may actually be the one who has already given one response since she still has one ticket to spend. This will happen only if the other two players have not raised their hands at all.

If a student correctly identifies the two words in the sentence that can be combined to form a compound word, she earns points as follows:

2 points if her first ticket is being spent
1 point if her second ticket is being spent
1 additional point for using the correctly identified
compound word in a meaningful sentence.

If the compound word has not been revealed after all tickets have been spent or after enough time has elapsed, ask for an answer from the class. Award no points in this case.

Repeat the above process by returning all tickets to the same three respondents. Read another sentence from the provided list. After two

or three different sentences, select a new respondent from each team and repeat the procedure. Continue as long as time allows making sure that each student has been a ticket holder at least once. The team with the most points at the end of play is the winner.

MODIFICATIONS: In upper grades, provide the student with a compound word, and award a point if he can formulate a sentence which includes both halves in "uncompounded" form.

Sentence List

I threw my ball to second base.	BASEBALL
He marked the board with blue chalk.	CHALKBOARD
Shine that light where she is headed.	LIGHTHEADED
Jamal put a tarp over the new board.	OVERBOARD
Check to see if you have your book.	CHECKBOOK
A maple tree grows beside our house.	TREEHOUSE
Be sure to walk around that broken board.	BOARDWALK
The lake seems to shine in the sun.	SUNSHINE
We'll have ham, bread and corn for dinner.	CORNBREAD
I heard my mare whinny last night.	NIGHTMARE
After her bath she put on her green robe.	BATHROBE
Hey, Bud, please pick me a rose.	ROSEBUD
Don't get in my way when I drive!	DRIVEWAY
Her swollen foot was completely bare.	BAREFOOT
Tamila walked down to the lower end of town.	DOWNTOWN
I read that book last year.	YEARBOOK
The ground under the tree was very hard.	UNDERGROUND
Baby Hal took enough steps to walk one foot.	FOOTSTEPS
That phone is too close to my head.	HEADPHONE
In their yard was an old grave.	GRAVEYARD
The heavy book fell off the shelf.	BOOKSHELF
Greta dropped her key down the hole.	KEYHOLE
The speeding car headed straight for our pig.	PIGHEADED

From their place they could see the fire.	FIREPLACE
During the storm we got six inches of snow.	SNOWSTORM
The dog took his stick to our neighbor's yard.	YARDSTICK
Last fall the water came over the bridge.	WATERFALL
Her pocket was filled with a book and an apple.	POCKETBOOK
Please pick up the spoon under the table.	TABLESPOON
Shuffle the cards and pin them to the board.	SHUFFLEBOARD
Her heart felt like it had broken into pieces.	HEARTBROKEN
The main battle took place on that rocky field.	BATTLEFIELD
My cat ate a mouse and two big fish.	CATFISH
Jill took wood from the porch to start a fire.	FIREWOOD
Come back in here and pack your luggage.	BACKPACK
Do you know where any of the kids went?	ANYWHERE
Put your cup and your dish in the pan.	DISHPAN
Jack stacked the lumber in the garage.	LUMBERJACK
They used a real horse in that play.	HORSEPLAY
Wear the socks that are under your bed.	UNDERWEAR
That little boy fed the cow with no help at all.	COWBOY
Julio had a patch on his cap and on his knee.	KNEECAP
Is there enough room to play cards in here?	PLAYROOM
Set this plant where it can get a little sun.	SUNSET
They went down the hall to count the votes.	COUNTDOWN
It's almost time to spring out of this chair.	SPRINGTIME
The group leaders asked us to give a big cheer.	CHEERLEADERS
The rain ruined the bow on the wreath.	RAINBOW
Tim saw the teacher with the gold chain.	CHAINSAW
That man nailed the announcement to the post.	POSTMAN
Comb the mustard and honey out of your hair.	HONEYCOMB
If you shake the milk, it might taste better.	MILKSHAKE
When we got home we made our own ice cream.	HOMEMADE
The playful dog ran all around that pile of wood.	DOGWOOD
Henri has gone where no other man has.	NOWHERE
Mother said not to step on the wet floor.	STEPMOTHER
Ada can make this cake in just a short while.	SHORTCAKE
Bring some scotch tape to the sock hop.	HOPSCOTCH

CONTRACTION ACTION

Students with word cards will search for words on cards held by others in an attempt to find pairs of words that can form contractions.

OBJECTIVES: Vocabulary
Contractions
Thinking

TARGET POPULATION: Grades 2 - 5
MATERIALS: Word Cards (To be copied)
Chalkboard and chalk; Tape
Contraction List (See appendix)

PROCEDURE: Shuffle the deck of word cards and deal one card to each student. The deck may be "stacked" so that students who need more practice with contractions receive cards with words that are more often contracted, such as "is" or "not". Each student reads his word and then tapes his card to his shirt so that others can easily read it.

Instruct students to simultaneously roam the room in search of other students' word cards to combine with their own to form a contraction. When a pair of students thinks that a contraction can be formed from their words, the two lock arms and raise their free hands. When several pairs are ready to respond call, "Freeze". All students must then stop and listen. Select one pair and point to the person who has the first word of the contraction. He says his word aloud. Then point to his partner who says his word aloud. Finally point to both of them, and they say their contraction in unison. If the class agrees that a legitimate contraction was formed, write it on the chalkboard. Repeat this procedure with all other arm-locking pairs. When all have finished say, "Resume", and all students, including those whose contractions have already been used, continue to search for new partners.

When most students appear stumped, have one of them point out each contraction on the board that was formed with his word. This will show that some words are contracted more often than others. When this student has finished, ask for suggestions from the class for additional contractions for that student's word. Write those on the board as well.

One at a time, call students to the chalkboard and repeat this process. Conclude the activity when all have finished.

MODIFICATION: Copy and pass out several cards for words that are more often contracted.

were	had	have
what	where	how
did	there	will
am	has	does
do	not	can

is	are	was
should	would	could
it	we	they
you	he	she
that	who	I

FOOTBALL CONTRACTS

Students will listen to a sentence and change two of its words into a contraction, or change the included contraction back to its 2-word form.

OBJECTIVES: Contractions, Vocabulary, Auditory association & memory Thinking

TARGET POPULATION: Grades 2 & above

MATERIALS: Sentence List (provided)
Chalkboard & chalk
Magnet or self-stick note

PROCEDURE: Divide the class into two teams, and assign each a football team's name. On the chalkboard draw a "football field" with ten 10-yardline markings. Place a self-stick note or magnet on the 50-yardline to represent the football. Write one team's name on each end of the field.

Explain to students that when it is their turn to respond they will stand. A sentence will be read that may or may not contain a contraction. If the sentence has a contraction, the student must repeat the given sentence, but change the contraction to its uncontracted form. For example, if the sentence is "I'll see you later", the student's response should be "I will see you later." If, however, there is no contraction in the given sentence, the student's job is to repeat the sentence with a contraction formed from two of the given words. For example, if the provided sentence is "*You have* been busy", the student's response should be "*You've* been busy."

Have the first person from one team stand. Read a sentence from the provided list, wait a few seconds, and repeat it. Do not emphasize the target word(s) when reading the sentence. Allow the student fifteen seconds to respond. If his answer is correct, move the football 10 yards closer to his team's goal. If he is incorrect, move the ball 10 yards in favor of his opponent, and ask for a volunteer from the class to provide the correct answer. Then have the first player from the opposing team stand. Repeat the process with a new sentence. Continue alternating in this fashion.

When either team reaches the goal line, it scores a touchdown worth six points. The player whose response advanced the team to the goal line is then eligible for the extra point attempt. Read that person another sentence from the list, and score one more point for a correct response.

Replace the football on the 50-yardline and begin again. Start with the team that did not last score. Continue for as long as time allows, and then declare the team with the highest score to be the winner.

MODIFICATIONS: Use two footballs and allow each team to progress toward its own goal. Return both balls to the 50-yardline after a touchdown.

Sentence List

He will draw another picture. (He'll)
Hector is the cat that has scratched the sofa. (that's)
After lunch I'm going to go shopping. (I am)
That's probably the best thing we could do. (That is)
Miranda could not stop the deer from eating her roses. (couldn't)
She is wearing the silliest hat today! (She's)
If you feed them now, you will be late for school. (you'll)
We shouldn't be in her yard now. (should not)
You must not drink so much soda pop. (mustn't)
Why do you not listen to me? (don't)
She does not have any friends. (doesn't)
I wouldn't try that right now. (would not)
James cannot eat any more pizza tonight. (can't)
I think he would be happy to help us. (he'd)
Please don't leave for home yet. (do not)
The fire truck didn't arrive on time. (did not)
What will they think about her new hairdo? (What'll)
I've never been to Hawaii. (I have)
Do you think we are the only ones here? (we're)
There was not much left to do. (wasn't)
I have never seen a dog like that before! (I've)
Won't Hank go to the game tonight? (Will --- not)
Mr. and Mrs. Colton did not plan to leave until 4:30 P.M. (didn't)
Her family can't afford a new car right now. (cannot)
The boys mustn't bother the old man across the street. (must not)
He's the right one to do this job. (He is)
Right now I am so tired that I might just fall asleep. (I'm)
Isn't there a rosebush in her back yard? (Is --- not)
Mr. Thomas said he was not sure about taking that new job. (wasn't)
Where's the ring that Joey bought for her? (Where is)
You have never liked her, have you? (You've)
They're the ones you should talk to about your problem. (They are)
We'll talk to your parents about the field trip. (We will)

DETECT 'VE

Students will write one contraction from a heavily loaded sentence.

OBJECTIVES: Contractions, Vocabulary
Strategies, Thinking
Auditory memory

TARGET POPULATION: Grades 2 & above
MATERIALS: Sentence List (provided)
Paper and pencil/student
Chalkboard & chalk

PROCEDURE: Divide students into several teams, and provide each student with a piece of paper and a pencil. If teams cannot be divided evenly, it will be necessary to declare someone from each of the "shorted" teams to be the "double respondent". This person can write two responses for each sentence in order to ensure that all teams are given an equal number of scoring opportunities. Teammates could take turns being the double respondent.

Explain that each student will be writing down one, *and only one,* contraction from the sentence that will be read. Points will be earned as follows: If a student writes a contraction from the given sentence, *and no more than three students from the class* have written that same contraction, each of the students with that response scores one point for his team. It is possible, therefore, that all of the points for a particular sentence will go to the same team. Explain to students that it is to their advantage to choose a contraction that they think few others will select. Copying a word that someone else has written will decrease the chances of earning points.

Read a sentence from the provided list three times so that no one must ask for repetition. When all students are ready with one written word begin checking responses. Slowly read the sentence again with a pause between words. When the student hears the teacher say the contraction that he has written, he must immediately raise his hand or be left out of the count. Tally each point as it is earned. Be sure to inform students which words are contractions in a sentence, even if no one has selected a particular one.

Continue by reading another sentence three times, and following the same procedure. When time runs out the team with the most points wins.

MODIFICATIONS: Deduct a point from a team if one of its members writes a word that is not a contraction in the given sentence.

Sentence List

I know that you'll like what we're planning, and that's guaranteed.
We're determining who isn't in the club, and who didn't even want to be.
Doesn't your sister know that she's the one they'll choose to be president?
He'll take us to see what's going on at that new place they're building.
Haven't you sensed all along that the kids didn't know that you're a preacher?
There's a reason why we couldn't find out who's in charge.
My aunt wouldn't have been angry if she'd seen how hard they'd worked.
You shouldn't have told Brad he's stupid because he doesn't understand this.
She's older now, but that's a secret that Dad still won't tell her.
She said you'd be upset if you weren't able to see who's playing in the game.
Weren't you relieved to learn that he'll be on the same team that you're on?
The boss hasn't bought the supplies that I'm suppose to use, so I'll buy my own.
I'd like to know who's responsible for the gossip you've been hearing.
It's been a long time since we've gone there, but there's a good reason.
You've got to tell me who's not where they're supposed to be.
Wasn't the boy whose cough wouldn't quit the same one you've been helping?
I don't care who's the boss, as long as it isn't Dale.
Everyone's been saying that you've been fired, but it isn't true, I hope.
We'd better tell Jeff that he'll be in charge if Matt doesn't show up.
I can't go until after she's done with her lessons, or she'll get upset.
I'm sure you'll love the CD they're putting out when their tour's over.
She hasn't noticed that there's a boy in her class who can't read.
I'm not sure if it's okay with Granny, or if she'll be upset with us.
She's gone away, and they're not sure when she'll return.
Nobody's been more concerned about how he's doing than I've been.
What's the math assignment that we're supposed to do while he's gone?
When the show's over we'll leave, and then he'll drive us home.

CONTENT WITH THE CONTENT?

Students will read given sentences and correctly pronounce the included heteronyms.

OBJECTIVES: Vocabulary
Teamwork
Strategies
Heteronyms

TARGET POPULATION: Grades 4 & above
MATERIALS: Chalkboard & chalk
Heteronym Sentence List (copy as needed/team)
Tickets (copy one/student from appendix)

PROCEDURE: Divide the class into teams of no more than four or five students, and give each student a ticket. Provide each team enough copies of the provided sentence list so that everyone can read one. (NOTE: Fold back the right edge of the sentence list before making copies for students.)

Announce the sentence group that will be used for round one. Keep students from working ahead on sentence groups by *not* going in numerical order. Teams will be given a predetermined amount of time, such as two minutes, to together read over the announced group. Students are to determine how heteronyms in the given sentences should be pronounced. All of the sentences should be practiced within the given amount of time.

When time expires allow no more conferring. Ask for a volunteer from Team 1 to read any one of those sentences, correctly pronouncing each of the heteronyms. If the student is able to do so, take his ticket and place the letter "H" on the chalkboard under "Team 1". The "H" is the first letter of the word "HETERONYM" which must be spelled in its entirety for a team to win. Correct or not, ask any player from Team 2 who wishes to respond to select another sentence to read. If both heteronyms are pronounced correctly, place an "H" under "Team 2" on the chalkboard, and take the respondent's ticket. Anytime an incorrect response is given, the student loses his turn, but not his ticket, and any other team may again try that sentence. Continue in this fashion from team to team awarding letters as earned. Only those students who have a ticket may raise their hands to respond.

A response will be considered to be incorrect if:

1) Either or both of the heteronyms in the sentence were pronounced incorrectly
2) A respondent receives help from a teammate after the conference time has expired
3) A respondent reads a sentence that has already been read correctly by any team (He may, however, read a sentence that was *incorrectly* attempted by any team)
4) A teammate who does not have a ticket gives a response
5) No one with a ticket wishes to respond.

Continue looking for a correct response for the first sentence group until all have been reveled or until two incorrect answers in a row have been given by each team. Then ask for volunteers from the class, including those whose tickets have already been spent, to supply correct pronunciations for the remaining heteronym sentences. Help students, if necessary.

Announce another sentence group to the class, and repeat the procedure. Only those students who still hold tickets may reply. When a team has successfully spent all of its tickets, give another to each member of that team only. Begin each round with the team that follows the last to answer correctly.

Continue the activity for as long as time allows, or until any team spells "HETERONYM". If no team completes the word "HETERONYM ", the team with the most letters wins.

MODIFICATIONS: Instead of having students read the sentences, read them aloud and have students identify the heteronyms in each.

Sentence List

(FOLD BACK HERE BEFORE COPYING)

GROUP 1	(pronunciation)
We all read the story that the teacher asked us to read.	(red, reed)
Take your final bow, and then tie a bow to hold the curtains back.	(bow, boe)
We live near a grocery store that sells live bait.	(liv, liev)
The doctor wound the bandage around the wound on my knee.	(wownd, woond)
Don't forget to polish the Polish furniture.	(PAH-lish, PO-lish)
The dove dove low to the ground to fly through the trees.	(duv, doev)
His crew couldn't wind the sail while the wind was so strong.	(wined, wind)
GROUP 2	
I shed a tear when I heard about the tear in the expensive painting.	(teer, tare)
The soldier decided to desert his station in the desert.	(de-ZERT, DEH-zert)
A number of injections by the dentist made my jaw feel number.	(NUM-ber, NUM-mer)
Get the lead out, and lead us to the hospital!	(led, leed)
That buck does not like to be too close to those does.	(duz, doze)
Why do we subject ourselves to talk shows about that subject?	(sub-JECT, SUB-ject)
If you can't digest that whole story, find it in the *Reader's Digest*.	(di-GEST, DI-gest)

(FOLD BACK HERE BEFORE COPYING)

GROUP 3

Our farm has to produce enough produce to feed four families.	(pro-DUCE, PRO-duce)
An invalid license was reported by the invalid.	(in-VAL-id, IN-va-lid)
The bass player caught the biggest bass at the fishing tournament.	(base, bass)
The boys refuse to take any more refuse to the dump.	(re-UZE, REF-use)
The workers asked Jeff to present the present to the boss.	(pre-ENT, PREZ-ent)
Close the door and sit close to me to get warm.	(cloze, close)
A seamstress and another sewer stumbled over the sewer line.	(soh-er, soo-er)

GROUP 4

Compress these herbs so we can make a compress for your head.	(com-PRESS, COM-press)
Did the coach contest the new addition to the team for this contest?	(con-TEST, CON-test)
Postal workers had to resort all the mail that blew across the resort.	(RE-sort, re-ZORT)
The scientists tried to perfect the vaccine to make it perfect.	(per-FECT, PER-fict)
You must project your voice while speaking about our project.	(pro-JECT, PRO-ject)
Dad tried to console him offer the vandal destroyed his console TV.	(con-SOLE, CON-sole)
At the last minute Mr. Collins brought up a minute point.	(MIN-it, my-NUTE)

GROUP 5

Did the sheriff record all of these counts on his record?	(re-CORD, REC-ord)
If you continue to progress like this, your progress will be amazing.	(pro-GRESS, PRO-gress)
Mom will not permit me to get a hunting permit.	(per-MIT, PER-mit)
The contractor is going to reside the house where my cousins reside.	(RE-side, re-ZIDE)
Resign yourself to the fact that we must resign the smudged papers.	(re-ZINE, re-SINE)
Don't reject my idea just because some reject told you to.	(re-JECT, RE-ject)
We reserve the right to reserve leftover food the following day.	(re-ZERV, re-SERV)

GROUP 6

Gayle and Lynn had to alternate being the team's alternate.	(ALL-ter-nate, ALL-ter-nit)
The proceeds of the fundraiser will be used as the project proceeds.	(PRO-seeds, pro-SEEDS)
Are you sure that you are content with the content of this movie?	(con-TENT, CON-tent)
I suspect that the police have a suspect in mind.	(sus-PECT, SUS-pect)
If we could teach our sow to sow, the planting would be much quicker.	(sow, soe)
The judge did not object to bringing the object into the courtroom.	(ob-JECT, OB-ject)
Go to this address, and help them address the letters.	(ADD-ress, a-DRESS)

WRITE RIGHT

Students will select appropriate homophone pairs to fit in sentence blanks.

OBJECTIVES: Homophones
Thinking
Vocabulary
Auditory memory & association

TARGET POPULATION: Grades 3 & above
MATERIALS: Homophone Pair List (provided)
Homophone Sentence List (provided)
Paper & pencil/team
Chalkboard & chalk

PROCEDURE: Divide the class into teams of 3 – 5 students. Select a recorder for each team and give her pencil and paper. Choose one group of homophone pairs from the provided list and write it on the chalkboard. Then read aloud one of the sentences from the corresponding sentence list saying, "Blank" for each of the missing homophones.

Teams must choose the correct homophone pair to complete the sentence. Recorders write their teams' choices on their papers in the correct order, such as "chute/shoot". After 30 seconds announce, "Pencils down."

Have each recorder tell the homophone pair chosen by her team. Scoring is done as follows:

1) If only one team has written the answer correctly, it scores *two* points for each team that is incorrect. For example, Team B scores 6 points because Teams A, C, & D are incorrect.

2) If two or more teams have the correct answer, each of these teams receives *one* point for each team that is incorrect. For example, Teams B, C, & D score one point each when Team A is wrong.

3) If *all* teams are either correct or incorrect, no team scores.

On the board cross off the homophone pair that was used. Read aloud another homophone sentence and follow the same procedure. Change recorders, if desired.

After six sentences have been read, ask for a volunteer to use the remaining homophone pairs in meaningful sentences. Then erase the list on the board and write another group for round two. Proceed with as many rounds as possible and then total all points. The team with the most wins.

MODIFICATIONS: Follow the same procedure but do not write homophone pair choices on the board.

HOMOPHONE PAIRS

GROUP 1
aisle-I'll-isle
eight-ate
bald-bawled
bare-bear
be-bee
beet-beat
blue-blew
bored-board

GROUP 2
guessed-guest
grate-great
hall-haul
heel-heal
here-hear
horse-hoarse
hymn-him
in-inn

GROUP 3
knew-new
knot-not
led-lead
mail-male
meet-meat
nose-knows
pail-pale
sea-see

GROUP 4
peal-peel
fur-fir
passed-past
time-thyme
scent-cent
rap-wrap
red-read
road-rod

GROUP 5
break-brake
bury-berry
but-butt
buy-by
cheep-cheap
clothes-close
daze-days
deer-dear

GROUP 6
peace-piece
do-dew-due
plane-plain
sail-sale
fare-fair
flu-flew
flower-flour
flee-flea

Sentence List

GROUP 1

The ___ man yelped when he cut himself and then he ___ for an hour. (bald/bawled)
Do you believe that Johann ___ more than ___ pounds of potatoes? (ate/eight)
I would ___ happier if that ___ weren't buzzing around my head. (be/bee)
If you are so ___, why don't you two play a ___ game? (bored/board)
The wind ___ the clouds across the ___ sky. (blew/blue)
I can't ___ to see him walk on the hot sand in his ___ feet. (bear/bare)

GROUP 2

We saw the ___ that George Washington slept ___. (inn/in)
We had to ___ that dresser all the way down the ___. (haul/hall)
Shane never ___ that he was the ___ of honor. (guessed/guest)
If you sit ___ , you'll be able to ___ the music perfectly. (here/hear)
The ___ that we sang reminded ___ of his childhood. (hymn/him)
I hope that sore on my ___ will ___ quickly. (heel/heal)

GROUP 3

I'd like to ___ someone else who eats no ___. (meet/meat)
The girl with ___ skin took a ___ to the beach. (pale/pail)
Harry ___ he has the largest ___ in his family. (knows/nose)
The guide ___ us all through the old ___ mine. (led/lead)
I'm glad that there is ___ even one ___ in your shoestrings. (not/knot)
Can you ___ that pelican flying out to ___? (see/sea)

GROUP 4

As I heard the bell ___ I slipped on a banana ___ and fell down. (peal/peel)
He ___ the sign in the back of the ___ truck. (read/red)
I wouldn't pay one ___ for something that had the ___ of a skunk! (cent/scent)
He ___ the go-cart on the dirt ___. (rode/road)
Ann wore her new ___ coat as she sat waiting under the ___ trees. (fur/fir)
Please ___ up this new CD of ___ music for Chad's birthday. (wrap/rap)

GROUP 5

Rover likes to ___ his bones under the ___ bushes. (bury/berry)
These ___ Mike seems like he's always in a ___. (days/daze)
The farmer went right ___ the feed store but forgot to ___ birdseed. (by/buy)
Finish putting away your ___ and then ___ your drawers. (clothes/close)
That small baby ___ is so ___ to those children. (deer/dear)
After just one day he managed to ___ the front ___ on his bicycle. (break/brake)

GROUP 6

Although she had the ___, the pilot ___ the plane to Mexico. (flu/flew)
It's not really ___ to charge such a high ___ for that taxi ride. (fair/fare)
Helen used ___ to mark the borders of her new ___ bed. (flour/flower)
Each child colored a small ___ of the ___ sign. (piece/peace)
The left side of the ___ looked ___ without any art work. (plane/plain)
I bought the cloth for this ___ at a fabric ___ last week. (sail/sale)

AWL OAR NUN

Students will formulate sentences that show an understanding of each word in a homophone group.

OBJECTIVES: Homophones
Vocabulary
Teamwork, Strategies

TARGET POPULATION: Grades 3 & above
MATERIALS: Homophone List (copy one/team)
Chalkboard & chalk

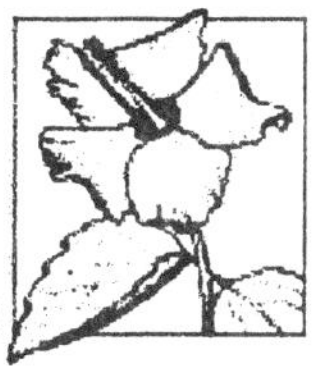

PROCEDURE: If possible, divide the class into 4 - 5 teams. Copy the homophone list and give one to each student. Explain that for a team to earn a point, it must correctly use each word of a homophone pair (or trio) in a sentence that shows an understanding of its meaning. For example, the following would be acceptable sentences for the homophone pair "knot, not": "I tied a knot in my shoelace", and "I am not going home." The sentence "I have a knot" is unacceptable since it fails to indicate whether the team understands the meaning of the word "knot". In this case give the team one more chance to be more specific.

Designate a spokesperson for each team. Teammates may suggest sentences for her to use, but the spokesperson is permitted to formulate her own sentences, if she wishes. Sentences are *not* to be written.

Instruct teams that only a specified group of homophone pairs (or trios) may be used at any one time. Select any eight pairs that are in order, such as the last eight pairs in the second column, and announce them to the class. Allow all teams a few minutes to discuss the meanings of the words in this selected group. Then announce that no more discussions may be held.

Begin by asking Team 1's spokesperson to identify the homophone pair that her team will attempt to explain. Then ask her to state her sentences. Determine ahead of time whether to require that the spokesperson spell which homophone is used in each sentence, or if simply giving two correct sentences is enough.

Scoring is done on an "all or none" basis. If both (or all three) of the sentences are acceptable, award one point to the responding team for *each* homophone used. If a spokesperson is unable to correctly use any or either of her homophones in a sentence, she receives no points and her team may not attempt that same homophone pair again. If a team does not receive points for its selected homophone group, any *other* team may try it.

Tally the points for Team 1, if any, on the chalkboard and ask the spokesperson from Team 2 to identify the homophone pair that it will attempt. Once again the words must be chosen from the same homophone group that was previously announced. Tally any points earned by Team 2 and then each of the other teams. Return to Team 1, 2... until all six of the homophone sentences for a particular group have been correctly identified or until each team has guessed all that it wishes or is allowed. Then ask for volunteers to formulate sentences that show the meanings of the remaining homophones in that group.

Resume the activity by designating another group of eight homophone pairs (or trios) and repeating the above process. Select a new spokesperson for each team. Begin with the team that follows the last to score.

When the desired amount of time has elapsed, the team with the most points is the winner.

MODIFICATIONS: For upper level students, select more difficult homophone pairs from the HOMOPHONE RESOURCE LIST in the appendix.

Require that *both* homophones be used in a single sentence.

Homophone List

knot/not
tease/teas
bass/base
right/write
mite/might
pray/prey
pier/peer
pair/pear
fined/find
awl/all
or/oar/ore
knight/night
reel/real
chews/choose
cellar/seller
loan/lone

nun/none
seize/sees/seas
horse/hoarse
road/rode/rowed
overdo/overdue
ceiling/sealing
week/weak
poor/pour/pore
great/grate
piece/peace
throne/thrown
made/maid
hour/our
course/coarse
do/dew/due
heard/herd

threw/through
tax/tacks
male/mail
paced/paste
board/bored
cite/sight/site
to/too/two
wait/weight
creek/creak
scent/sent/cent
scene/seen
chili/chilly
mall/maul
sum/some
heel/he'll/heal
chute/shoot

EYE SEIZE A PEAR

Students will identify the homophone pair in an oral sentence.

OBJECTIVES: Vocabulary
Homophones
Auditory memory & association
Thinking

TARGET POPULATION: Grades 1 & above
MATERIALS: Number cards (copy/team from appendix)
Homophone Pair Sentence List (provided)
Chalkboard & chalk

PROCEDURE: Divide the class into three or four teams. Within each team shuffle the number cards from 1 to the number of students on the largest team, and give one card to each student. For example, if there are six players on the largest team, give each team the number cards from 1 - 6. It does not matter which player gets which number. Give one player on each of the "shorted" teams a leftover number card.

When each player has his card, randomly announce one of the numbers and write it on the board. Anyone who is holding that number, one from each team, stands. Standing students are the only ones permitted to respond and teammates may not assist in any way.

Tell students to listen for a homophone pair in the sentence that will be read. One standing student will earn points for his team by being the first to call out the intended homophones. For example, in the sentence "John ate all eight of the doughnuts", the first standing person to shout, "Eight" is awarded one point for his team. Each standing player gets one guess only, so if he is incorrect, he is finished. After a homophone pair is identified have all standing students sit. Announce another number and write it on the board. Everyone holding that number now stands.

Continue reading sentences for round one until every player's number has been called. Then ask each team to collect, shuffle, and redeal its own cards. Different groups of standing students will now be formed. To expedite this process, consider awarding an extra point to the team that gets ready first.

Continue playing for as many rounds as time allows and then total all points. The team with the most points is the winner.

MODIFICATIONS: ⚑ ♈ ● ⚐ ♒ ♌ ❖ ✌

Sentence List

When we go to church I'll sit in the seat by the aisle.

Joe ate all eight of the doughnuts.

The wind blew the clouds across the bright blue sky.

I read that book with the red leather cover.

Thomas, close the door to your clothes closet.

Rover likes to bury his bones under the berry bushes.

I have a blister on my heel that I hope will heal quickly.

Vlad said we would not have enough wood for the entire project.

I forgot to pay the tax when I bought those tacks for you.

Adam will write a speech to give kids the right message.

Not one male in the class has received any mail this year.

We need to fill this hole with a whole bunch of gravel.

She accidentally threw the ball right through the front window.

Ginnie can sew very well, so why doesn't she fix your shirt?

When we went on vacation we stayed in the fanciest inn I've ever seen.

The farmer bought a water hose, two rakes, and three hoes.

Kareem ducked to avoid hitting his head on the heating duct.

Last week when my uncle was ill, he felt weak for days.

There is no way that I am going to let you see how much I weigh.

Don't stare, but check out the guy standing on the top stair.

Their parents were married in that chapel over there.

There was a good piece in the newspaper about the peace talks in Bosnia.

I've been thinking about getting a new recycling bin.

The pirates will seize all the gold from other ships on the high seas.

If you drive by the drug store, please stop and buy me some cough syrup.

Mix flour, water, and food coloring, and then shape the dough into a flower.

I am not going to untie the knot in your shoelaces one more time!

We had to haul the old sofa up the steps and down the hall.

I don't think Meg knew that we were getting another new student.

Use the telescope to see the dolphins jumping in and out of the sea.

Bring along some board games to keep from getting bored.

The boys rode the horses through the fields, over the hill, and down the road.

Tosha and Ned will stay here and call us when they hear the buzzer go off.

Gram has a great soup recipe, but she has to grate pounds of carrots.

Rams like to fight and butt the other goats, but I think they're really cute.

Although my voice is hoarse, I can still ride my horse this afternoon.

I asked Jim if he would meet me at the old gym.

HEAR A RIDDLE HERE

Students will include a pair of homophones when restating a definition or sentence.

OBJECTIVES: Homophones, Synonyms
Vocabulary, Humor
Auditory association
Teamwork, Strategies

TARGET POPULATION: Grades 3 & above
MATERIALS: Chalkboard & chalk
Homophone Riddles (provided)

PROCEDURE: On the chalkboard draw the following chart:

1	2	3	4	5

Easiest---------------Hardest

Divide students into two teams. Within each team make several subgroups of two or three. It does not matter how many subgroups have two and how many have three, as long as each team has the same number of groups.

Choose a subgroup from each team to stand for round one, and select a spokesperson for each. Seated subgroups may not assist. Inform standing students that they are to think of a pair of homophones to fit a given definition or to restate a sentence. Provide the following examples to help students understand:

1) pretends to be a hatchet-like instrument (acts like an ax)
2) a precious fawn (a dear deer)
3) a visitor took a chance at the answer (a guest guessed)

Allow the spokesperson from Team 1 to select a number from 1 - 5. Explain that a "1" selection indicates an easier riddle, a "2" is a little harder,... and "5" the most difficult. If correct, students will earn the number of points that the puzzle is rated. Choose a riddle from the provided list that matches the selected number. Read the riddle and give a predetermined amount of time, such as 20 seconds, for both standing groups to confer. When time expires allow the spokesperson from Team 1 to respond first.

If Team 1 is incorrect or has no answer, allow Team 2's spokesperson to give an immediate guess. If correct, Team 2 collects the point value for that riddle. If Team 2 is also incorrect, neither team earns points. Ask for a volunteer to give the correct answer, or simply reveal it.

Continue the procedure with the same two subgroups, but this time ask the spokesperson from Team 2 to choose a point value from 1 - 5. Team 2 will respond first to this new riddle.

Once this riddle has been revealed, ask the next subgroup from each team to stand for round two. Continue the above procedure with two riddles per round until all groups have had a turn. Start again, but this time change the order so that no subgroup is competing against the same opponents. Select a new spokesperson for each group.

Once all of the riddles of a particular level have been given, cross that number from the chart on the board. Continue as long as time allows, and then total all scores. The team with the most points is the winner.

MODIFICATIONS: ♒ ⚐ ⚐ ● ♌ ✋ ✍ ▭

Homophone Riddles

(NOTE: Answers may be phrased differently than those provided and still be correct.)

LEVEL 1:

Cookie batter for a female deer - *Dough for a doe*
A naked grizzly - *A bare bear*
To look at the ocean - *See the sea*
Mailed him a penny - *Sent him a cent*
To be introduced to a hamburger - *Meet the meat*
Prepared by the house servant - *Made by the maid*
Two yellow fruits - *A pair of pears*
To print correctly - *Write right*
Letters for boys - *Male mail*

LEVEL 2:

Mailed her some perfume - *Sent her a scent*
An inexpensive bird noise - *A cheap cheep*
What a doctor hopes to do - *He'll heal*
A worn-out red vegetable - *A beat beet*
To look intensely at the step - *Stare at the stair*
Traveled on the highway - *Rode the road*
Listened to a group of cows - *Heard the herd*
To sneak a look at the mountaintop - *Peek at the peak*
A beany soup that's gotten cold - *Chilly chili*

LEVEL 3:

A feeble seven days - *A weak week*
A daisy made of dough - *A flour flower*
To lift up the sun's beams - *Raise the rays*
To shut the bag on the garments - *Close up the clothes*
Took a plane ride while sick - *Flew with the flu*
The fur of the bunny - *The hair of the hare*
A tiny insect that can run away quickly - *A flea that can flee*
To pin the T-bone to the ground with a stick - *Stake the steak*
A rainbow over Noah's boat - *An arc over the ark*

LEVEL 4:

A solar offspring - *A son of the sun*
A large tree with smooth bark on the ocean shore - *A beech on the beach*
An authentic piece of fishing apparatus - *A real reel*
The king was knocked off his chair - *He was thrown from his throne*
The doctor's clients waited quietly - *The patients had patience*
A four-legged animal with near-laryngitis - *A hoarse horse*
To murder Santa's vehicle - *Slay his sleigh*
The dog's feet stop for a moment - *His paws pause*
Sixty minutes for you and me - *Our hour*

LEVEL 5:

An Indian corn puzzle - *A maize maze*
Precipitation during the king's rule - *Rain during his reign*
A donkey who can dig up the ground - *A burro who can burrow*
She was sorry the fog was gone - *She missed the mist*
Carry a heavy load down the corridor - *Haul it down the hall*
A weird fair - *A bizarre bazaar*
To make money from the predictor - *Profit from the prophet*
Waterproofing a room's top surface - *Sealing the ceiling*
An ape-like army fighter - *gorilla guerilla*

HUMOR ME

Students will answer riddles that are based on multiple meaning words.

OBJECTIVES: Multimeaning words (Homographs)
Creativity
Vocabulary

TARGET POPULATION: Grades 2 - 6
MATERIALS: Riddles List (provided)
Chalkboard & chalk
Paper & pencil/team

PROCEDURE: Divide students into teams and give each team paper and pencil. Have one person from each team stand and prepare to respond to a riddle which will be read aloud. Explain that each riddle will be based on a multiple meaning word and remind students that riddles have answers that are considered to be humorous, often making sense in a silly way.

Choose one riddle from the list to read aloud as an example. Before revealing the answer choices, however, ask if anyone would like to guess. Then explain how points will be earned. Students who respond correctly earn three points for answering a riddle *before* the three answer choices are provided, or one point if the choices have been given. Finish the example, explaining the humor, if necessary.

Begin by reading another riddle from the provided list. Each standing student who thinks she knows the answer without hearing the three response choices writes her guess on her paper and turns it face down on her desk. Students who have not written a response continue to hold their papers.

Reread the riddle this time providing the three answer choices. Everyone who is still holding her paper writes an answer now. Students who have already guessed may also choose to change their answers now. Classmates are not allowed to assist.

Then ask each student who kept the response that she wrote *before* hearing the answer choices to reveal her answer. Tally three points for each acceptable answer, *even if it is different than the one provided.* Next ask those who responded *after* hearing the three choices to state their selections. Reveal the correct answer and explain, if necessary. Tally one point for each of those correct responses.

Have a different student from each team stand for round two and proceed as above. Continue with as many rounds as possible, making sure that every player has the chance to respond once before allowing any student a second turn.

When time expires total all points. The team with the most points wins.

MODIFICATIONS: ✋ ❄ ⌘ ⚐ ❖ ♒ ♈ ●

Riddles

(The word in *italics* is the multiple meaning word on which the riddle's humor is based.)

What has *eyes* but cannot see?
a. bugs [b.] needles c. birds

What father is as sweet as candy?
a. fireman [b.] lolli*pop* c. police

What has four *legs* but cannot run?
a. camel b. cow [c.] table

What has *hands* but cannot feel?
a. gorilla b. nurse [c.] clock

What kind of house is never heavy?
[a.] *ligh*thouse b. birdhouse c. doghouse

What kind of building keeps the sky clean?
a. barn [b.] sky*scraper* c. burning house

What does a dog do that a boy wears?
a. runs [b.] *pants* c. shirt

What does a flag do to say "good-bye"?
a. droops b. flaps [c.] *waves*

What word usually has one *letter* only?
a. it b. I [c.] envelope

What kind of *driver* doesn't use a car?
a. race driver [b.] screw*driver* c. teenager

What has 4 wheels and *flies*?
a. a Jeep b. a helicopter [c.] a trash truck

What animals are used in baseball?
[a.] *bats* b. monkeys c. goose

What has a *tongue* but cannot speak?
a. mouth [b.] shoe c. boy

What color can you peel?
a. green b. purple [c.] *orange*

What has a *roof* that never gets rained on?
a. shed [b.] mouth c. bicycle

What month is in a parade?
[a.] *March* b. June c. May

What do you use to fix a broken pizza?
a. super glue [b.] tomato *paste* c. tape

What follows *tracks*, but never leaves any?
a. bear b. policeman [c.] train

What has a *head and a tail*, but no body?
[a.] a penny b. a dog c. a boy

What *runs* day and night, but goes nowhere?
[a.] clock b. lizard c. horse

What *room* is too small to enter?
a. bathroom b. kitchen **c.** mush*room*

What kind of cat doesn't purr?
a. tiger **b.** *cat*fish. c. lion

What dessert does a stonecutter like best?
a. applesauce b. ice cream **c.** *marble* cake

Why does the frog have no more friends?
a. They left home. **b.** They all *croaked.*
c. They're mad at him.

What do cheerleaders like to drink?
a. *root* beer b. lemonade c. iced tea

How do you find a spider on the Internet?
a. Have him paged. b. E-mail him.
c. Go to his *web* site.

Why didn't the owl get mad?
a. He didn't give a hoot. b. He didn't care.
c. He was sleeping.

Which snakes are best at math?
a. rattlesnakes **b.** *add*ers c. copperheads

What famous person can be seen in the sky?
a. a pilot **b.** a *star* c. an astronaut

What is a frog's favorite year?
a. Y2K b. next year **c.** leap year

Where do strawberries play music?
a. at a concert b. in a park **c.** at a *jam* session

What do you call a cat that eats lemons?
a. a sour *puss* b. lemon face c. silly kitty

What kind of *table* has no legs?
a. a kitchen table b. a cafeteria table
c. a multiplication *table*

Why did the ham go to the doctor?
a. to be eaten b. He was sick. **c.** to get *cured*

Where do bugs like to do their shopping?
a. at the supermarket **b.** at the *flea* market
c. at the shoe store

What does the trash man like to eat?
a. apple pie **b.** *junk* food
c. spaghetti and meatballs

Where do hamburgers get to dance?
a. at school b. at a show **c.** at a meat*ball*

What is the funniest card in the deck?
a. the *joker* b. the king c. the ace

MULTIMEANING@dot.dot

Students will tell possible meanings of an ambiguous sentence caused by multiple meaning words.

OBJECTIVES: Vocabulary
Ambiguity
Multimeaning words (Homographs)
Strategies

TARGET POPULATION: Grades 2 & above
MATERIALS: Dot-to-dot Grid (copy from appendix)
Ambiguous Sentence List (provided)
Marker

PROCEDURE: Hang the dot-to-dot grid where everyone can see it, or draw a similar grid on the chalkboard. Divide the class into 3 - 4 teams and assign each a team number.

Read to the class an ambiguous sentence from the provided list. Emphasize the word that is written in *italics.* Ask the first player from Team 1 to tell one meaning for the ambiguous sentence. If his explanation is satisfactory, he may draw a line between any two vertical or horizontal adjoining dots on the grid. Teammates may not instruct him as to the placement of the line and once a student begins drawing he may not decide to change its location. Without waiting for the line to be drawn, continue the activity.

If the first player was incorrect in his explanation of the ambiguous sentence, he connects no dots. Regardless, move on to the first player of the next team and ask for an unrevealed explanation of the same ambiguous sentence. If this player restates the same meaning that the first player already gave, explain, and allow him one more chance to give a new explanation. If he is incorrect, ask in order the first player from each of the other teams, and then the second players. . . until at least one failed attempt has been made by each team. If no one provides the correct response, ask for volunteers but award no points.

Two meanings of the ambiguous sentence must be exposed before moving on to a new sentence. Depending on the skill level of the class, however, decide whether a third, or fourth definition must also be given (when one exists). Otherwise, simply tell students the additional meanings.

Reveal the next ambiguous sentence and begin with the person who follows the last to answer correctly. As each student gives a correct response he is permitted to connect horizontal or vertical dots on the grid. The object of connecting the dots is for each team to complete as many "boxes" as possible. Each time a box is completed the team member who drew its fourth side writes his team's number inside the box. It may be pointed out to students, or left for them to discover for themselves, that putting the *third* side on the box may not be in their best interest. This allows the next correct respondent to complete a box. For example:

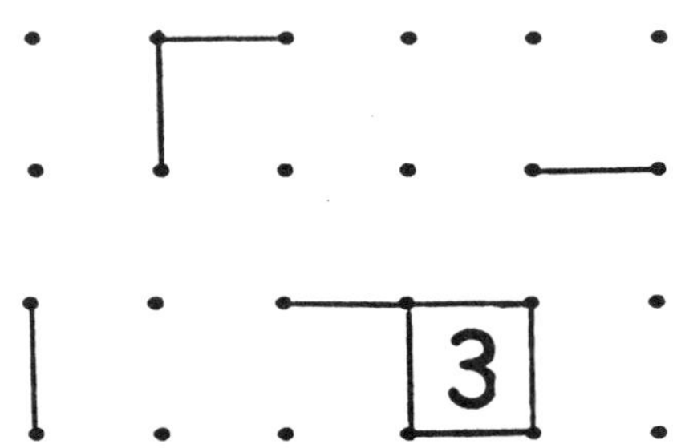

Continue revealing ambiguous sentences until everyone has had a turn, or until time expires. Then count the number of boxes that each team has completed. The winning team is the one with the most boxes.

MODIFICATIONS:

Sentence List

I hope no one else sees this *spot.*	(soiled place; certain area)
The gray *trunk* was very rough looking.	(elephant part; tree base; storage unit)
The *nut* fell out of the tree.	(bolt's partner; food; silly person)
The puppy ran around the *block.*	(chunk of wood; city square; child's building toy)
Can you *sign?*	(write one's name; use sign language)
There was a huge *tank* in the yard.	(large container; armored, military vehicle)
We saw a picture of his *chest.*	(body part; trunk)
She forgot her *slip* today.	(undergarment; piece of paper)
The *band* made her head hurt.	(musical group; wrap-around strap)
This *cold* is keeping me at home.	(low temperature; illness)
Mr. Gomez needs a new *pen.*	(small, enclosed area; writing tool)
I noticed that he has a large *bill.*	(beak; payment due)
Dharma can't get her *part* right.	(hair division; actor's lines; section)

He passed out after that *shot.*	(injection; gunfire; throw of a ball)
One *foot* is way too long.	(body part; linear measurement)
Keisha sprayed water on her *palm.*	(part of hand; plant)
Stay away from that *kid!*	(young goat; child)
Will we need to have a *drill?*	(practice; tool)
They're playing in the *spring.*	(season; coil; ground water)
How did you break that *nail?*	(hammer's partner; part of a finger)
The inspector found a *bug* under the table.	(listening device; insect)
Nathaniel has a special *gift.*	(talent; present)
The *rest* will do her good.	(nap; remainder)
Mom took the box to the *nursery.*	(baby's room; plant-growing business)
Try to find another *match.*	(fire-stick; go-together; competition)
The *seal* was a shiny black color.	(flippered animal; closure; embossed stamp)
Do we need a new *pitcher?*	(beverage container; ball thrower)
The *fans* are expected by two o'clock.	(air moving devices; great admirers)
They are really *rich!*	(wealthy; full of fats & sugar)
Shane has only half of a *tablet* left.	(pill; pad of paper)
Alexei put on another *coat.*	(outer garment; layer of paint)
Ask Lottie for a *date.*	(escort; fruit; calendar division)
Carlie bought some *bulbs* at the store.	(light-up devices; parts of a flower)
That isn't very *bright.*	(well-lit; smart; having hot colors)
Bart talked a lot about his new *case.*	(storage container; work assignment; furniture)
Who put this *check* on the table?	(bank draft; check mark; checkered pattern)
It was a very *cool* day.	(temperature; fun)
Marvin said it was a *snap.*	(easy; kind of noise; clothing closure)
Jeff really needed that *change.*	(modification; coins)
I've seen Carter *draw* a gun before.	(pull out; make a picture of)
Was there a *fork* in the road?	(eating utensil; split in a roadway)
The *walk* was way too long.	(pathway; travel by foot)
He wasn't happy with the *tie.*	(same ending score; neckwear; knotting)
Annie said it had three *stories.*	(tales; floors of a building)
Stay away from that *horn!*	(trumpet; antler; car noisemaker)
Her *calf* was injured.	(lower leg; baby cow)
Those *glasses* were already broken.	(eyewear; drinking vessels)
Does Mom have any *dough?*	(batter; money)

TIC TAC TWO

Students will identify and define multiple meaning words that appear in sentence pairs.

OBJECTIVES: Vocabulary, Thinking
Auditory association & memory
Multimeaning words (Homographs)

TARGET POPULATION: Grades 2 & above
MATERIALS: Sentence Pair List (provided)
Chalkboard and chalk

PROCEDURE: Draw a tic tac toe grid on the chalkboard and divide the class into Team "X" and Team "O". Ask one player from Team X to stand. Read a pair of sentences from the provided list. The standing player's job is to name the multiple meaning word that was used in both sentences. If he is correct, he must then give a brief definition or explanation of the word as it was used in each sentence. If he successfully does so, he then selects a square on the tic tac toe grid for his team's mark.

If the standing player is incorrect in identifying the multiple meaning word from the sentence pair, the first player from Team O is given a chance at that same pair. If a standing player correctly identifies the multiple meaning word, but is unable to provide its meaning in each of the given sentences, ask for a volunteer to do so. In this case neither team puts its mark on the tic tac toe grid.

If a mark is won, begin the next sentence pair with the opponent. If neither team earned a mark for the last pair, begin with the team that did not have first chance the last time. Play passes back and forth until one team has recorded three horizontal, vertical, or diagonal marks in a row on the grid. Begin again, if time allows.

MODIFICATIONS: A 4 x 4 grid may be used that would require either four marks in a row or a mark in each of the four corners to win.

Read the sentence pair with blanks in place of the multiple meaning words, and have players choose the appropriate word to complete both blanks.

Sentence Pair List

Dad gave me a buck for some candy.
Deep in the woods I saw a buck.

We need to grade our driveway.
What grade did you get on the test?

I love to fly kites in March.
The drummer likes to march in parades.

We saw a crab scurry under that rock.
I wish Blair would stop being such a crab!

My brother and I joined the same club.
She had one club and six spades in her hand.

Do you like to bowl?
There's some fruit in the blue bowl.

You'd better duck quickly!
We saw a male duck in the pond.

The sugar cane grew very high last summer.
Grandpa's cane is hand-carved.

Be careful where you step.
The next step is to color the eggs.

The cook was grouchy all day.
Let's cook some spaghetti tonight.

He tires easily since he's been ill.
Tom needs two new tires.

Craig likes to row for exercise.
Everyone in the third row may get a drink.

The snake shed its skin in our barn.
Put the rakes in the old shed.

Will sent a post card to his aunt.
Uncle Joe wrote his will last year.

Dad got a new leather coat.
The walls need another coat of paint.

Circle the correct answer.
The silly dogs ran around in a circle.

I'll feed these seeds to the birds.
The horses like their new feed.

Court will recess for one hour.
I'll meet you out on the court.

Roll up your sleeping bags now.
I'd like my sandwich on a roll.

I'll change out of my wet clothes.
How much change will you get?

That fly is sure annoying!
I love to watch the bats fly overhead.

Mary is a very patient lady.
The patient groaned in her sleep.

Her purple dress was torn.
Dress the doll in your old baby clothes.

Where can we hide the money?
Julian was paid $20 for each deer hide.

Don't squash that spider!
We enjoy raising squash in the garden.

Her dad works at the chemical plant.
In the spring I love to plant flowers.

Use a clip to hold those papers together.
I'll clip the dog after lunch.

The doctor said his heart is very weak.
Johann drew a heart with Leah's name inside it.

Dad will pick us up after the game.
Can you pick that lock?

The kind old man gave me a ride.
What kind of ice cream do you want?

The sink was full of dirty dishes.
The old rowboat might easily sink.

Were you present when he gave his speech?
I'll bring you a present when I return.

Circle the right answer for each problem.
Turn right just past the church.

Do you think the rain will last all week?
He was the last in line to get tickets.

Set the dishes on the table for me.
I bought a new set of tires last week.

Don't trip on that loose piece of carpet!
Mr. and Mrs. Ling are on a trip to Mexico.

Cinderella left the ball in a hurry.
Marta, throw me that small blue ball.

I have a hunch that he'll leave home.
Hunch over you so can fit under the porch.

He threw a punch at the other boxer.
She served us punch with fruit in it.

The poem is on page 133 of the blue book.
I'll page the doctor as soon as I can.

We bought some land near the river.
The helicopter will land on the ball field.

After you cut your hair, wash it.
Clean out that cut on your leg.

I have three dogs and a horse to train
The train on her gown was stained.

We need all of you to back up a little bit.
Hogan painted the back of his house.

Let's eat lunch in the park.
She prefers to park her car in the lot.

We all rose to our feet and cheered.
Denzel sent her a beautiful yellow rose.

The wallpaper won't stick to the wall.
If I throw this stick, my dog will fetch it.

The Maxwells bought a two-story home.
That was truly an amazing story.

MULTI-TWO'D

Students will name one multiple meaning word that suits two definitions.

OBJECTIVES: Vocabulary
Multimeaning words (Homographs)
Auditory association & memory
Thinking, Strategies

TARGET POPULATION: Grades 3 & above
MATERIALS: Definition List (provided)
Chalk & chalkboard
Number cards (copy 1 set/team + 1 set/teacher from appendix)

PROCEDURE: Divide students into teams of up to six members. Write each team's number in a different space on the board. Shuffle one set of number cards 1 - 6 (or 1 - 5, if there is a maximum of 5 players per team) and pass them out to players from Team 1. Shuffle the other sets and deal one to each of the other teams. If teams do not have equal numbers of players, give one player from each of the "shorted" teams two different number cards. Each team will, therefore, have one player with a #1 card, one player with a #2 card... When round one is finished, select different students to hold two cards.

Shuffle the teacher number cards and randomly draw one. Announce the drawn number to the class. Anyone who is holding that number, one person from each team, must stand. Only those who are standing may respond, and sitting students may not assist.

Explain to students that two brief definitions will be given. Both definitions refer to the same word. Students are to determine the one word that fits those definitions. For example, "a crazy person" and a "bolt's partner" both define a "nut". When a standing player thinks he knows the answer he raises his hand. Call on the first to do so. If incorrect, however, he may not guess again for that clue.

Read a pair of definitions for a multimeaning word from the provided list. Select the first, if any, hand-raiser to respond. If his response is correct put an "H" on the chalkboard under each of the *other* teams' numbers. The "H" is the first letter of the word "HOMOGRAPH" (multimeaning word). The object of this activity is to NOT earn letters on the board. Each time a player answers correctly, he may choose whether to add one more letter to each of the other teams or to erase one letter from his own team. If no standing student is able to give a correct response, no team is given a letter. One player must get the answer right before other teams are penalized.

After the first correct response is heard, have standing students sit. Draw another number from the teacher's pile of cards to allow new players to stand. Read another pair of definitions and repeat the above process.

Once all numbers have been called, collect each team's cards and redeal them. Each student will now have a good chance of competing against different opponents.

Continue the activity until time expires, or until any team spells "HOMOGRAPH" in its entirety. The team with the fewest letters on the board is the winner.

MODIFICATIONS: ❄ ⌘ ❖ ♈ ♒ ⚐ ♌ ● ✌ ▭

Definition List

A male deer; one dollar (buck)
Breathes heavily; trousers (pants)
12 inches; body part with a heel (foot)
To jog quickly; a small creek (run)
To punish by beating; a short oar (paddle)
A drinking tube; hay-like grass (straw)
Business organization; guests (company)
A dog's noise; tree covering (bark)
Finger jewelry; a circus circle (ring)
A time of year; to add flavor (season)
Well kept grassy area; 3 feet (yard)
One-fourth; a coin (quarter)
Type of metal; tool to reduce wrinkles (iron)
A writing tool; fenced animal area (pen)
A duck's beak; account of money due (bill)
To crowd together; jelly (jam)
A student; the black part of the eye (pupil)
For no cost; at liberty (free)
A kind of bird; to gulp (swallow)
A tree's body; car's storage space (trunk)
Part of a minute; before third (second)
An alphabet piece; a written note (letter)
An organization; a wooden weapon (club)
Earth's atmosphere; an opening (space)
A vegetable; to flatten (squash)
A king; a measuring stick (ruler)
Part of the hand; a tropical tree (palm)
Unable to see; a window covering (blind)
Not heavy; not dark (light)
A ball thrower; beverage container (pitcher)
Smart; very shiny (bright)
A go-together; fire-stick (match)
A season; water from the ground (spring)
Boring; not sharp (dull)
Baseball player; pancake mixture (batter)
A tall bird; a lifting machine (crane)
A spinning toy; a shirt (top)
To intersect; irritable (cross)
To punch someone; foot clothing (sock)
To look at something; a timepiece (watch)
Level and smooth; divisible by 2 (even)
To motion "bye"; an ocean's swelling (wave)
To obey; the brain (mind)
Military rank; important (major)
Maybe; power & strength (might)
An underground hollow; to collapse (cave)

DOUBLE OR NOTHING

Students will fill the blanks in a given sentence pair with the same multiple meaning word.

Objectives: Multimeaning words (Homographs)
Auditory memory & association
Vocabulary
Teamwork

TARGET POPULATION: Grades 2 & above
MATERIALS: Sentence Pair List (provided)
Chalk & chalkboard
Paper & pencil/team

PROCEDURE: Divide the class into teams of small numbers that can easily confer. Designate a recorder for each team and give her paper and pencil.

Tell all students that they are to think of target words that can fill the blanks of sentences that will be read. For a response to be correct it must fit appropriately into the given sentence, and *must be a word that has more than one meaning*. Choosing a response such as "me" for example, is not a good choice since "me" has only one meaning.

Select a sentence pair and ask any class member whether she wants to hear sentence "A" or sentence "B" first. Read the requested sentence, and allow all teams time to confer. Recorders should write one multimeaning word (homograph) that could appropriately complete the blank. When recorders are ready they should stand. Do not yet reveal the correct answer.

Read the second sentence of the pair. Each team may now choose either to keep its original response, indicating that the previously chosen word also fits the second sentence, or to change its original response to one that will fit both of the revealed sentences. Repeat both sentences several times so that no one must ask for repetition. After a sufficient amount of conference time, announce, "10 seconds more". Then award points as follows:

1) If a team's first answer was correct and is kept as its final choice, award 2 points.
2) If a team's first answer was incorrect, but the final answer is correct, award 1 point.
3) If for any reason the final answer is incorrect, award no points.
4) If a team has no written answer, award no points.

Choose another sentence pair, and again ask any classmate if she wants to hear sentence "A" or "B" first. Read that sentence and continue as above. When time expires, total all points. The team with the most points wins.

MODIFICATIONS: ▭ ⚐ ♈ ● ♌ ❖

Sentence Pair List

RUN
A. Can you ___ to the store for me?
B. Don't let the water ___ all night.

CASE
A. Put that knife in its ___.
B. I'll take an umbrella in ___ it rains.

TURN
A. Be careful as you ___ that key.
B. Whose ___ is next?

TRAIN
A. Jim took the ___ to New York.
B. Al can ___ a dog to jump a fence.

SPOT
A. With a scope I can ___ a deer.
B. Eve got a ___ on her new skirt.

COAT
A. Her ___ has a fur collar.
B. Todd put a ___ of paint on the door.

BASE
A. Remember to tag the ___.
B. Let's sit at the ___ of the tree.

RIGHT
A. Turn ___ at the corner.
B. Your father is always ___!

HANDLE
A. The mug's ___ is hot.
B. ___ that antique carefully.

KIND
A. What ___ of car did your sister get?
B. The old man was ___ to his neighbors.

RING
A. For her birthday Jennie got a ___.
B. Can you hear those church bells ___?

HOSE
A. Her ___ had a run in them.
B. Turn on the water ___, please.

MOUTH
A. Zack put the carrot in his ___.
B. The cave is by the ___ of the river.

LIGHT
A. My backpack is not ___.
B. Mom turned on the ___ in my room.

FACE
A. Which way should the chair ___?
B. Ben always has a smile on his ___.

SPOKE
A. The bike wheel has a broken ___.
B. Anna ___ to the waiter.

FEET
A. My ___ are really sore.
B. That room is sixteen ___ long.

PLANT
A. My dad works at the power ___.
B. The flowers on that ___ are beautiful.

SAW
A. She ___ Jesse at the theater.
B. He picked up the hammer and ___.

YARD
A. There is a rabbit in the ___.
B. She bought a ___ of cloth.

STALL
A. My dad's car might ___ again.
B. I put the horse in the ___.

WELL
A. I don't feel ___ today.
B. Don't drop the bucket down the ___.

CIRCLE
A. A ___ has no straight sides.
B. ___ the right answer on your paper.

PRESENT
A. Santa left a ___ under the tree.
B. I'll call roll to see who is ___.

PIN
A. ___ this badge on your shirt.
B. I left only one bowling ___.

CAN
A. Open a ___ of soup for me.
B. I know you ___ do this math.

FLY
A. That annoying ___ is still buzzing around.
B. Andrew learned how to ___ a plane.

CHANGE
A. I need to ___ my shoes.
B. Do you have enough ___ for a soda?

ROLL
A. My dog likes to ___ down the hill.
B. I'll have a ___ and some cheese.

SAND
A. Dad wants to ___ that wooden table.
B. Ben played in the ___ at the beach.

SHED
A. Did your snake ___ its skin?
B. The rake is in the tool ___.

STEP
A. She fell off the bottom ___.
B. I will ___ off the ladder carefully.

DRESS
A. That's the perfect ___ for the prom.
B. ___ the baby warmly to go outside.

SOCK
A. I can't find the mate to this ___.
B. The bully will ___ you if he sees you.

PARK
A. You can't ___ in that driveway.
B. Let's have a picnic in the ___.

BOWL
A. Would you like a ___ of chili?
B. I will learn to ___ tonight.

PATIENT
A. The doctor expected his next ___.
B. Please be ___ and quiet.

TRIP
A. Don't ___ on that wire.
B. How was your ___ to Alaska?

TWO OR MORE

Students must spell the correct plural form of a given word.

OBJECTIVES: Plurals
Strategies
Vocabulary

TARGET POPULATION: Grades 2 & above
MATERIALS: Word List (provided)
Chalk & chalkboard

PROCEDURE: Divide the class into Team "X" and Team "O". On the chalkboard draw a 3 x 3 grid for a tic tac toe game. Label each of the nine boxes of the grid with one of the singular nouns from the list below.

Have one person from Team X come to the board and choose the box where she would like to place her team's mark. She reads aloud the word in that box and then states and spells its correct plural form. Some students might prefer to write the new word on the board rather than to spell it aloud. If her response is correct and so is her spelling, she may enter her team's mark in the selected space. If the student responds incorrectly, either by stating the incorrect plural form or by incorrectly spelling it, she does not earn her mark. Do *not* yet reveal the correct spelling since one of the teams may attempt it later. Correct or not, play passes to the opponent who may try to earn any of the empty spaces on the grid.

Be sure that every team member has one turn before anyone gets a second. The first team to get three marks in a row wins the game.

MODIFICATIONS: ✋ ❄ ⚐ ❖ ♒ ♈ ⚐ ♌ ●

Word List

thief (thieves)	deer (deer)	beach (beaches)	porch (porches)
watch (watches)	dish (dishes)	wolf (wolves)	class (classes)
mix (mixes)	brush (brushes)	tax (taxes)	body (bodies)
story (stories)	foot (feet)	calf (calves)	church (churches)
leaf (leaves)	shelf (shelves)	kiss (kisses)	body (bodies)
glass (glasses)	box (boxes)	arch (arches)	knife (knives)
man (men)	wish (wishes)	sheep (sheep)	alley (alleys)
lady (ladies)	child (children)	moose (moose)	loaf (loaves)
tooth (teeth)	woman (women)	life (lives)	crash (crashes)
mouse (mice)	fox (foxes)	baby (babies)	elf (elves)
goose (geese)	wife (wives)	fly (flies)	die (dice)
witch (witches)	ash (ashes)	bus (buses)	reindeer (reindeer)

PLURALITY

Students will identify the correct and incorrect plural forms of given nouns.

OBJECTIVES: Plurals
Vocabulary
Auditory association

TARGET POPULATION: Grades 2 - 5
MATERIALS: Noun List (provided)
Chalkboard and chalk
[1] & [2] cards - (copy 1 set/student from appendix)

PROCEDURE: On the chalkboard write the numbers 1 - 50, and the following answer key:

[1] = YES

[2] = NO

Ask any student to pick a number from 1 - 50. Cross his choice off the chalkboard so that no one else will select it. Read the noun beside the student's number from the provided list. Ask the student to say what the plural form of the noun would be if it were formed by adding only an "s" or "es". For example, if the noun is "child", the student should respond with "childs". He then thinks of a sentence for his new plural noun, and tells it to the class. ("The *childs* went to the circus.")

All students will then individually decide if "childs" is the correct plural form of "child". Each student who thinks the plural form was correct will prepare to hold up his [1] card ("YES"). Each student who thinks the form was incorrect will prepare to hold up his [2] card ("NO"). Students should avoid letting others know which card they have selected. This can be accomplished by placing the selected card on top of the other card and then holding both together against the chest.

When all students are ready say, "Raise your cards", and all students should do so simultaneously. No student may change his response after viewing the cards of others. It is now possible to see which students are having difficulty with plurals.

Inform students of the correct answer card and, if necessary, ask a volunteer to state the correct plural form. Make up a new sentence with the appropriate plural form.

Continue play by choosing another student to select a number from 1 - 50, and proceeding as above.

MODIFICATIONS: This activity can be played in a game format by dividing the class into teams with equal numbers of players. Individuals who respond correctly score points for their teams.

Noun List

1. dress
2. prince
3. gift
4. leaf
5. letter
6. bench
7. chair
8. tooth
9. child
10. monkey
11. chief
12. gas
13. lily
14. card
15. man
16. knife
17. calf
18. carpet
19. suitcase
20. boy
21. rash
22. shelf
23. wife
24. tomato
25. book
26. foot
27. radio
28. bridge
29. witch
30. tax
31. jelly
32. goose
33. girl
34. moose
35. hallway
36. house
37. life
38. table
39. fox
40. shoe
41. potato
42. woman
43. bag
44. shirt
45. thief
46. cage
47. mouse
48. ox
49. apartment
50. soldier

(Add "s" or "es" to underlined words to form plurals.)

BACK TO BASICS

Students will identify the base word that is common to two given words.

OBJECTIVES: Base words
Prefixes, Suffixes
Auditory memory & association
Vocabulary, Thinking

TARGET POPULATION: Grades 2 & above
MATERIALS: Word Pair List (provided)
Chalkboard & chalk

PROCEDURE: Divide the class into two teams. On the chalkboard draw the following diagram with as many steps as desired. Place an "X", one for each team, beside each of the bottom steps.

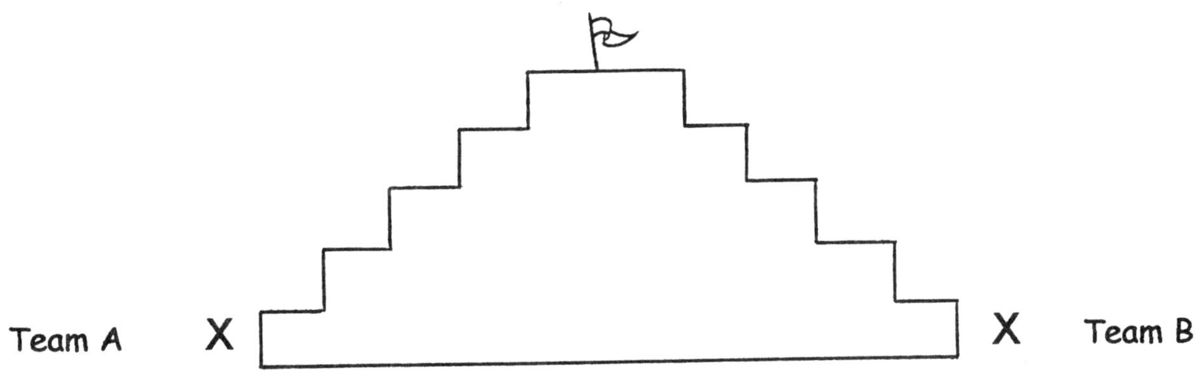

Begin with Team 1 and read to the first player a word pair from the provided list. This player is to state the base word that both of the given words contain. If the player is correct, place an "X" on the *first* step of Team 1's side of the diagram. If the player was incorrect, allow the first player from Team 2 to respond to the same word pair. Place an "X" on the next step of the team that finally answers correctly. If after two tries each, neither team is correct, ask for a volunteer to give the answer, but advance no "X" on the steps.

Choose a new word pair, and continue alternating teams. The first to reach the flag at the top of the steps wins. If time allows, begin again.

MODIFICATIONS: Require each correct respondent to use one or both of the two given words in a sentence before advancing his "X".

Require each correct player to name another word that uses the same base word before advancing his team's X.

Word Pair List

EASIER

unlikable, likeness (like)
agreement, disagreeable (agree)
especially, specialty (special)
reteach, teacher (teach)
midwest, western (west)
discover, uncovered (cover)
filling, refillable (fill)
childish, children (child)
careful, uncaring (care)
kindness, unkindly (kind)
artistic, artist (art)
distasteful, tasty (taste)
beautify, beautician (beauty)
unforgettable, forgetful (forget)
washable, unwashed (wash)
misfortune, fortunately (fortune)
replant, planter (plant)
unstoppable, stopped (stop)
painter, unpainted (paint)
strangely, stranger (strange)
uneasy, easily (easy)
usually, unusual (usual)
erasers, erasable (erase)
misleading, leader (lead)
loneliness, alone (lone)
disappear, appearance (appear)
mistreat, treatable (treat)
doing, redo (do)
discolored, colorful (color)
trainer, untrainable (train)
repot, potting (pot)
lacings, unlaced (lace)
sickness, sickly (sick)
incomplete, completely (complete)

MORE DIFFICULT

prehistoric, historical (history)
pressure, compressed (press)
shepherd, sheepish (sheep)
activity, reaction (act)
nonsmoker, smokeless (smoke)
himself, selfishly (self)
relationships, relatives (relate)
unbreakable, breakfast (break)
flaming, flammable (flame)
inhuman, humanity (human)
misbehaved, behavior (behave)
meaningless, meaningful (mean)
transform, formula (form)
electrical, electrician (electric)
irresistible, resistant (resist)
signature, unsigned (sign)
displeased, pleasant (please)
unjust, justify (just)
apartment, partition (part)
decision, undecided (decide)
continuous, discontinued (continue)
studied, students (study)
modification, unmodified (modify)
reassigned, assignment (assign)
replacement, displaced (place)
enforcement, forceful (force)
judgmental, judging (judge)
invitation, uninviting (invite)
detective, undetectable (detect)
placement, replacing (place)
provisions, providing (provide)
denote, notation (note)
thoughtfully, thoughtless (thought)
ownership, disown (own)

unDETECTable

Students will write one word that contains a prefix and/or a suffix from a heavily loaded sentence.

OBJECTIVES: Prefixes, Suffixes, Base words
Vocabulary, Thinking
Auditory memory & association
Strategies

TARGET POPULATION: Grades 3 & above
MATERIALS: Sentence List (provided)
Chalkboard and chalk
Paper & pencil/student

PROCEDURE: Divide students into teams and make sure that each person has paper and pencil. If teams cannot be divided evenly, it will be necessary to declare someone from each of the "shorted" teams to be the "double respondent". This will ensure equal scoring opportunities for each team. The double respondent can write two answers each time. Change the double respondent periodically or after each sentence.

Explain that each student will be writing down one, *and only one,* word that contains a prefix and/or a suffix from the sentence that will be read. Students will be working independently, but scoring points for their teams. Points will be earned as follows: If a student writes a word which contains a prefix and/or a suffix in the given sentence *and no more than three students from the class* have chosen that same word, each of the students who has written that word scores one point for his team. It is possible, therefore, that all of the points may go to the same team. The only exception to the "three or fewer" scoring rule is as follows: If a student writes a word that contains *both* a prefix and a suffix, she earns a point for her team no matter how many other students have chosen that same word. Explain to students that it is to their advantage to write a word with both a prefix and a suffix, or to choose a word that they think few others will select. Copying a word that someone else has written will decrease the chances of earning points.

Read a sentence from the provided list three times so that no one must ask for repetition. When all students are ready with one written response, begin checking. Read the sentence again with a pause between each word. When the student hears the teacher say the word that he has written, he must immediately raise his hand or be left out of the count. Tally each point as it is earned. Be sure to inform students which words in the sentence contain prefixes and/or suffixes even if no one has selected a particular one. Also, explain why incorrect responses are so.

Continue by reading the next sentence three times and following the same procedure. When time expires the team with the most points wins.

(Note: In the provided sentences plural words are included as words with suffixes. Although "s" is indeed a suffix, these words may be excluded from the choice of responses so that students do not always choose a plural word as an easy answer.)

MODIFICATIONS: Deduct a point from a team if one of its members writes a word that does not contain a prefix or a suffix.

Ask responding students to identify the base words in their choices.

Sentence List

A poisonous snake slowly disappeared under the rock where a lioness was sleeping.
The class misunderstood the directions that the teacher had explained earlier.
Tell the construction worker not to misplace his personal tools while using them on this job.
The heroism displayed by the freedom fighters was totally amazing!
Is it illegal for the ruler of that kingdom to be dethroned by our government?
Unfortunately the caterer miscalculated the number of expensive meals to be eaten.
A grayish cast filled the skies as the beautiful musical performance began.
The Spanish instructor is both likable and helpful, but I wish she were less talkative.
The overanxious pianist went quickly to buy extra supplies for his recital.
My ex-husband got a particularly mysterious phone call that offended him.
The hospital reported that a known alcoholic mistakenly took an overdose of medication.
The mighty river current was ultimately responsible for the deaths of three children.
The postal carrier thoughtfully resealed the invitation that my nosey brother had opened.
Some lovely trees were replanted in our apartment complex after the devastating storms.
If you continually misbehave and disobey me, you will earn unsatisfactory grades in conduct.
The passive bystander was powerless as a masked robber held up the First National Bank.
Should we discontinue reading the unedited nonfiction story written by that aging sailor?
The impatient artist hurriedly drew a smaller copy of that famous, colorful painting.
Last spring the American Medical Society mailed out discouraging information to smokers.
The farmer's field of soybeans was blackened by a spell of frosty nights earlier this month.
The teenagers who responded to the announcement were rewarded with free pizza.
The pre-kindergarten student insists on acting like the teacher's assistant.

BEFORE & AFTER

Students will decide if a given word includes a suffix, a prefix, or both.

OBJECTIVES: Vocabulary
Suffixes, Prefixes
Base words
Thinking

TARGET POPULATION: Grades 2 & above
MATERIALS: Word List (provided)
[1], [2], & [3] cards (copy 1 set/student from appendix)
Chalkboard & chalk

PROCEDURE: Give each student a [1] card, a [2] card and a [3] card. On the chalkboard write the following answer key for the number cards:

1 = BEFORE (prefix)   2 = AFTER (suffix)   3 = BOTH (prefix & suffix)

Instruct students that holding up a [1] card indicates that they have chosen "BEFORE" (prefix) as an answer, [2] means "AFTER" (suffix), etc. Make sure that all students understand this correspondence by asking them to hold up the card that means "BEFORE"... When students are ready, begin the game.

Read aloud a word from the provided list. Instruct students that they are to determine if the given word has a prefix BEFORE the base word, a suffix AFTER the base, or BOTH a prefix and a suffix. For example, if the chosen word is "beautiful", students who understand the instructions and the concepts will prepare to hold up their [2] cards ("AFTER"). Each student holds the card that reflects his answer against his chest to prevent others from viewing it. His unused number cards should be turned face down on his desk.

When all students are ready say, "Raise your cards", and all students do so simultaneously. No student is permitted to change his selection at this point. It is now easy to identify those students who are having difficulty understanding prefixes and suffixes. Ask for a volunteer to identify the base word and the affix(es) in the given word.

Continue the activity for as long as desired with other words from the provided list.

MODIFICATIONS: This activity can be played as a game by dividing the class into teams. Points can be earned by individual team members responding correctly, or by the spokesperson of the group being correct when reporting its consensus. If individual players are scoring points for their teams, be certain that all teams have an equal number of players, or assign "extra" players the task of judging the correctness of responses.

Extra points may be awarded for identifying the base word, and/or for using the word correctly in a sentence.

Word List

(after) beautiful
(after) longingly
(both) unhealthy
(both) reloaded
(both) unhappily
(before) discharge
(before) unsure
(after) lettering
(after) cleanest
(before) midnight
(before) immature
(after) crabby
(after) agreement
(after) lovable
(both) prepackaged
(both) uncertainty
(both) reaction
(after) shyness
(before) rematch
(after) circulation
(before) decode
(before) disgrace
(after) recently

(after) awesome
(before) midweek
(before) dishonest
(after) homeless
(both) unknowingly
(after) hopeful
(before) defrost
(after) projection
(both) biweekly
(before) update
(both) impersonation
(before) nonstop
(after) dangerous
(before) untie
(before) semicircle
(after) sloppiness
(both) replacement
(after) yellowish
(after) thoughtfully
(both) regrouped
(both) unbraided
(after) mighty
(before) untie

(after) privately
(both) reactivate
(after) allergic
(both) misfired
(after) greenish
(after) rental
(before) overfeed
(both) nonsmoking
(before) precook
(after) creative
(after) painful
(both) unloaded
(after) baroness
(before) recalculate
(both) impartially
(before) malcontent
(before) realign
(after) paraded
(both) disengaged
(before) submarine
(before) illegal
(after) chewy
(after) pavement

Tri-LINE-ing UP

Students will add a prefix to a given base word, a suffix to another, and then use both in a single logical sentence.

OBJECTIVES: Base words, Vocabulary
Prefixes, Suffixes
Sentences, Strategies

TARGET POPULATION: Grades 3 & above
MATERIALS: Base Word List (provided)
Affix List (provided)
Chalkboard & chalk

PROCEDURE: On the chalkboard draw a 4 x 4 (or 5 x 5) grid as pictured below. Print four base words from the provided "ADD A PREFIX" list across the top of the grid, one above each of the spaces. Print four additional base words from the provided "ADD A SUFFIX" list to the left of the grid, one beside each space.

(ADD A PREFIX)

(ADD A SUFFIX)	make	do	run	see
sad				
agree				
care				
act				

Divide the class into Team "X" and Team "O". Teams will take turns trying to win squares on the grid. The first team to complete a horizontal, vertical, or diagonal line with its symbol wins the game.

On the chalkboard write a list of prefixes and suffixes suggested by the class. Add extras, if desired, from the provided lists.

Ask the first player from Team X to choose the square that she would like to win. Teammates may not instruct the player as to which square to choose for a specific strategy. To win the chosen square the player must add a prefix to the base word above the column, a suffix to the base word beside the row, and use both of the new words in a single, meaningful sentence. For example, if the words are "make" and "care", an appropriate sentence would be "Ernest will remake the bed carefully", or "Don't be careless when you remake the movie." If a student is unable to use both words in their extended forms in a single, logical sentence, she does not earn the square.

After a sentence is stated, allow the opposing team to determine if it is correct. If so, the correct respondent puts her team's mark in the chosen space. Correct or not, play then passes to the other team.

Repeat the procedure with teams attempting to align four of their marks in a row. If neither team is able to do so, there is no winner.

MODIFICATIONS: To make this activity more challenging for upper grade levels, the same words can be used across and down the grid. Be certain to use words that can accept both a prefix and a suffix.

Allow a team to steal an opponent's square by stating a correct sentence with two *different* correct responses.

Base Word List

ADD A PREFIX

make	place	cook
view	like	cover
treat	do	match
locate	run	tie
mark	plant	behave

ADD A SUFFIX

slow	noise	care
beauty	soft	back
thank	agree	break
sad	sing	act
believe	quick	dress

Affix List

Prefix List

re-	dis-	in-
un-	fore-	under-
pre-	post-	over-
non-	out-	mis-

Suffix List

-ful	-less	-est
-er	-y	-ness
-ed	-tion	-ly
-ment	-ing	-able

(See PREFIX/SUFFIX RESOURCE LIST in the appendix for more suggestions.)

WAY OFF BASE

Teams will expand a given base word by adding a prefix(es) and/or a suffix(es).

OBJECTIVES: Base words, Vocabulary
Prefixes, Suffixes
Teamwork
Strategies

TARGET POPULATION: Grades 3 & above
MATERIALS: Paper & pencil/team
Chalkboard & chalk
Base Word List (provided)

PROCEDURE: Divide the class into teams of 4 or 5 students and select a recorder for each. Give each recorder paper and pencil.

Write one of the base words from the provided list on the chalkboard. Explain to the class that each team will add prefixes and/or suffixes to that base word to write *two* expanded words. Teams should write words that they think no other team will duplicate exactly. For example, if the base word is "light", each team may write any two of the following: "lights", "lightning", "lighten", "lighters", "enlighten", "lighting", "relight", "lightly", "enlightened"...

After about twenty seconds announce, "Pencils down", and begin checking answers. Checking may be done in either of two ways:

1) Have recorders simultaneously write their teams' responses on the board.
2) Ask each team in succession to orally report its reponses.

Anytime a team has written <u>exactly</u> the same response as another team, no team earns credit for it. Only unduplicated answers earn points. The words "lighter" and "lighters", for example, are considered to be different responses. Before beginning, however, it may be announced that "s", although indeed a suffix, may not be used as the *sole* suffix in this activity so that creativity will be encouraged.

Each time a team discovers that it has duplicated another team's response, all teams cross that word from its list. After all answers have been revealed, ask each recorder to restate its remaining correct word(s). Award one point for each.

Change recorders, if desired, and write another base word from the list on the board. Repeat the above procedure.

Continue this activity as long as time allows and then total all points. The team with the most points wins.

MODIFICATIONS: Write several base words on the board for students to expand within a given amount of time.

Base Word List (and examples)

EASIER

CLEAR	(clearly, unclear)
USE	(misuse, useful)
LOCK	(unlock, locker)
HELP	(helpless, helper)
LEAD	(mislead, leader)
ACT	(react, actress)
SAVE	(savings, savior)
PLAY	(replay, players)
CHARGE	(rechargeable, discharge)
SLEEP	(sleepless, asleep)
SAFE	(safety, unsafe)
OPEN	(unopened, opener)
NIGHT	(nightly, midnight)
PRINT	(reprint, printer)
COLOR	(discolored, coloring)
LIGHT	(relight, lightly)
DRESS	(undress, dresser)
EASY	(uneasy, easily)
HAPPY	(unhappy, happily)
WRINKLE	(unwrinkled, wrinkly)
CHANGE	(unchanged, changeable)
HAND	(handy, handful)
SPEAK	(unspeakable, speaking)

MORE DIFFICULT

ATTRACT	(unattractive, attraction)
APPEAR	(disappear, appearance)
DIRECT	(redirect, directions)
CALCULATE	(miscalculated, calculations)
MUSIC	(musician, musical)
TIME	(untimely, timeless)
ALLOW	(disallow, allowance)
PERSON	(impersonate, personality)
CLOSE	(disclose, closing)
CERTAIN	(uncertain, certainly)
THINK	(unthinkable, thinking)
REGULAR	(irregular, regularity)
SENSE	(sensible, nonsense)
PRODUCE	(reproduce, production)
TASTE	(distasteful, tasty)
SEASON	(preseason, seasoning)
TREAT	(mistreat, untreatable)
LOVE	(unloved, loveable)
DEVELOP	(undeveloped, development)
FORM	(deformed, formally)
JUDGE	(misjudged, judgment)
PART	(partition, particle)
PROVE	(improved, disprove)

BASE WORD BINGO

Students will identify words with prefixes and/or suffixes in sentences presented orally.

OBJECTIVES: Vocabulary, Base words
Prefixes, Suffixes
Auditory association
Thinking

TARGET POPULATION: Grades 3 & above
MATERIALS: Sentence Lists (provided)
Bingo Grids (copy one/student)
Pencil/student

PROCEDURE: Give each student a copy of the Base Word Bingo grid which includes a list of thirty base words. Tell students to complete their individual grids by writing one word from the list in each of the twenty-five squares. They may choose whichever words they want, and write them in any square. Each grid prepared in this manner should be unique.

When students have completed their grids, instruct them to listen to the sentence that will be read. Each sentence will include *two* words with a prefix and/or suffix. Students should mentally identify the two words and then determine their base words. If on their individual bingo grids students have written one or both of those base words, they mark an X in the square where those words appear. For example, in the sentence "The dog was playful in the beautiful meadow", the words "playful" and "beautiful" are both expanded words whose bases appear in the provided list. Students who have included "play" and/or "beauty" in their grids should mark those squares with an X. Slowly repeat the sentence two or three times. Keep track of the base words that have been read to make it easier to check for potential winners.

The game proceeds as above with additional sentences from the same sentence list. The first student to mark four base words in a row vertically, horizontally, or diagonally calls, "Bingo". Ask that student to name the four words that she marked to earn the win. Check to make sure that those base words were indeed used in the teacher-read sentences.

Play continues until three or four other students have achieved bingo. Students who have already won should continue to try for a second win.

MODIFICATIONS: Bingo grids can be reused for a second game by having students mark with a crayon instead of a pencil. A second sentence list is provided.

The game could be played in pairs with two students sharing bingo grids. This will help students who have difficulty functioning independently.

If the game seems too difficult for students, devise sentences that contain only one target word each.

Sentence List 1

Sentence	Base words
There was a playful dog in the beautiful meadow.	(play, beauty)
That movie is a remake of an old scary film.	(make, scare)
The precooked rice was loaded with salt.	(cook, load)
You need to rethink your last statement.	(think, state)
The soldier retreated to a safer spot.	(treat, safe)
She transplanted the flower carefully.	(plant, care)
The man rechecked the musical score for an error.	(check, music)
It is unbelievable that I misplaced my wallet again.	(believe, place)
Please redo the table setting.	(do, set)
I love seeing the unspoiled snow.	(see, spoil)
Marty worked slowly to finish his job.	(work, slow)
Jan dislikes the lamp on your dresser.	(like, dress)
He misbehaved his entire childhood.	(behave, child)
She looked for the letter that he enclosed.	(look, close)
His running style was the funniest I ever saw.	(run, fun)

Sentence List 2

Sentence	Base words
I was too scared to appreciate the beautiful old house.	(scare, beauty)
He was remaking the box for the musician's horn.	(make, music)
He acts funny when he's playing in the band.	(fun, play)
All of the children were outrunning me.	(child, run)
Granny overlooked a great place to settle down for a nap.	(look, set)
Have you seen my checkered shirt?	(see, check)
Don't be careless as you unload the back of the truck.	(care, load)
After working hard, Kirk undressed and went for a swim.	(work, dress)
She believed that she could cross the bridge safely.	(believe, safe)
Harsh treatment is necessary for that kind of behavior.	(treat, behave)
Our view was spoiled by the placement of that billboard.	(spoil, place)
She restated that she would have a huge planting of corn.	(state, plant)
Slowly he crept closer to the edge of the cliff.	(slow, close)
It is unlikely that your brother overcooked the stew.	(like, cook)
I was thinking about doing my homework right now.	(think, do)

Base Word Bingo Grid

Base Word Bank

look	play	safe	care	child	state
cook	dress	check	run	behave	close
place	plant	music	treat	believe	slow
beauty	like	scare	see	set	work
do	make	load	spoil	fun	think

BASE COMMAND

Students will state whether a given word contains a prefix and/or a suffix.

OBJECTIVES: Base words
Prefixes, Suffixes
Teamwork, Thinking
Vocabulary

TARGET POPULATION: Grades 3 & above
MATERIALS: Basic Training List (provided)
Badges (copy one/team)
Chalkboard & chalk, Tape

PROCEDURE: Read the following script to the class: "The Base Command is an elite group of starfighters whose job is to make certain that all captured Lexicons are reduced to their basics, and to send each part of each Lexicon to the appropriate Destination Station. Any trainee at Base Training who is unable to successfully complete his assignment will not earn his stripes, and will, therefore, be rejected from the Corps."

Divide the class into three or four bases (teams). Choose one person from each group to act as Base Commander and give him a badge. Send all Base Commanders to an area where they can easily confer. Designate a "rejection area", or tell students that if they are "rejected", they are to sit on the floor near their seats.

Read a word from the provided list to the first player from Team 1. Without advice from teammates, this player must state the base word in the given training word, and then the prefix and/or suffix, if any. All Base Commanders then confer to determine if the response was correct. If there is disagreement among the Commanders, the final decision is made by the one who was originally a part of the responding team. This Base Commander announces whether the given response was correct, in which case the respondent continues his basic training, or incorrect, in which case the respondent is rejected from the Corps and is sent to the rejection area.

The same procedure is continued with the first player from each team. Continue with the second players... until the activity is concluded.

Function as "General" in keeping control of the Base Commanders. If a Commander makes an incorrect decision, and incorrectly rejects or fails to reject a trainee, thus showing that he himself does not know the basic rules, he is relieved of his duties, and is sent to the rejection area.

Replace him with a non-rejected trainee from his team.

Round one of the activity is over after a few responses are received from each team. The end of each round is an arbitrary decision made by the General based on the number of students in the rejection area who need to get back into training. At the end of each round, record on the board the number of rejected trainees from each team. These numbers represent the total years necessary for each Basic Training Group to complete its assignment. More years may be added as additional rounds of the game are played.

Begin round two with the player who would have been next in round one. Continue play as described. When the final round has been played, calculate the total number of years necessary for each team to complete basic training. The winner is the team that will graduate first (with the least number of points).

MODIFICATIONS: To keep Base Commanders from intentionally giving bad advice to the Base Commander who is ultimately responsible for a decision, the General may decide to sentence each team to an extra year when any Base Commander makes an incorrect decision.

Basic Training List

(Prefixes and suffixes are underlined.)

unsatisfied	reapplying	hurried	departing	flooded	readers	eagerness
disconnect	watering	illegal	slowly	generally	picture	masterful
carpet	disappointed	painfully	advisor	diagnose	distrustful	unusually
treasure	encyclopedia	negative	angel	announce	language	rejection
misquoted	remind	graphics	window	instructions	improper	incompletely
practice	allowance	disappear	mistake	enlistment	eagerness	listen
unequal	lonesome	behavior	charming	prince	straight	journalist
improperly	preapproved	nightly	virus	container	hatchet	vacation
envelope	prayer	spinning	basic	farmer	microphone	reality
nondairy	ungraceful	straight	charming	number	imported	slumber
rejoin	reasonable	highest	midstream	creepy	poisonous	malnourished
folder	playful	Mexican	bubbly	beautiful	specialist	replacement

BADGES

RHYME TIME

Students will state a word that rhymes with a given word and fits a given category.

OBJECTIVES: Rhymes
Classification
Vocabulary
Auditory association & memory

TARGET POPULATION: Grades 1 - 5
MATERIALS: Watch w/ second hand (optional)
Rhyme Time Clue List (provided)
Chalkboard & chalk

PROCEDURE: Divide the class into 2 - 4 teams. Tell students that a clue will be read for a word that they are to guess. The clue will tell them the category that the word fits, as well as a rhyming word. An example would be: "Tell me a color that rhymes with fellow". The object of the activity is to *quickly* come up with a response. A correct response will earn points as follows:

Response time:	Point value:
5 seconds	3 points
10 seconds	2 points
15 seconds	1 point

Have the first player from Team 1 stand. Give her a clue from the provided list and begin timing. The student may make as many guesses as she wants within the 15-second time limit. If she is correct, check the chart and award her team the earned number of points. If she is incorrect, or if the 15-second time limit expires before the answer is given, ask for an immediate response from the next team's first player. If she is incorrect, continue asking the first player from each of the other teams until the correct response is finally given. If one player from each team has had the opportunity to respond, and has not been correct, reveal the answer. (Note: If only two teams have been formed, allow two players from each team to respond to a particular clue before revealing the correct answer.)

After the first answer is revealed, ask the next team's player to stand. Read his Rhyme Time clue and continue as above. Play as described until time expires. Then total all points and declare the team with the most to be the winner.

MODIFICATIONS: ⚑ ✋ ♈ ❖ ♌ ♒ ⚐ ●

Clue List

"Tell me a (kind of) _____ that rhymes with _____."
(Responses other than those in parentheses may exist)

color --- fellow (yellow)
animal --- sat (cat)
dairy food --- silk (milk)
boy's name --- games (James)
vehicle --- grain (train)
weather word --- proud (cloud)
number --- heaven (seven, eleven)
appliance --- drove (stove)
type of home --- sailor (trailer)
vehicle --- strike (bike)
sticky stuff --- waste (paste)
musical instrument --- suit (flute)
furniture --- head (bed)
camping gear --- bent (tent)
shape --- fair (square)
coin --- lime (dime)
tree --- lurch (birch)
car --- board (Ford)
farm equipment --- cow (plow)
color --- think (pink)
playground toy --- bride (slide)
drink --- joke (Coke)
planet --- stupider (Jupiter)
appliance --- poster (toaster)
fruit --- reach (peach)
musical instrument --- middle (fiddle)
baby animal --- half (calf)
gemstone --- made (jade)
animal's home --- rest (nest)
fruit --- Helen (melon)
creepy crawler --- rider (spider)
metal --- win (tin)
shape --- dart (heart)
clothing --- melt (belt)
beverage --- spruce (juice)
Santa's reindeer --- stupid (Cupid)

barnyard animal --- creep (sheep)
grain --- twice (rice)
baby animal --- mitten (kitten)
baked item --- fake (cake)
bird --- beagle (eagle)
coin --- Lennie (penny)
school subject --- mystery (history)
vegetable --- horn (corn)
floor covering --- bug (rug)
fabric --- rotten (cotton)
part of a car --- liar (tire)
planet --- pattern (Saturn)
insect --- cloth (moth)
month --- spoon (June)
body part --- harm (arm)
color --- clown (brown)
book --- kernel (journal)
precipitation --- pail (hail)
footwear --- gates (skates)
vehicle --- muggy (buggy)
car --- steep (Jeep)
furniture --- label (table)
state --- train (Maine)
farm animal --- wrote (goat)
flower --- hose (rose)
school subject --- path (math)
coin --- pickle (nickel)
metal --- mold (gold)
body part --- cart (heart)
vegetable --- wash (squash)
creature --- wagon (dragon)
month --- starch (March)
season --- dumber (summer)
body part --- colder (shoulder)
footwear --- dipper (slipper/flipper)
bird --- carrot (parrot)

MATCHMAKER

Students will write a word that rhymes with a given word, attempting to duplicate one of the three rhymes that a teammate records.

OBJECTIVES: Rhymes
Auditory association
Vocabulary

TARGET POPULATION: Grades 1 - 5
MATERIALS: Rhyming Word List (provided)
Paper & pencil/student
Chalkboard & chalk

PROCEDURE: If possible, divide students into teams of four or more and give each person a piece of paper. Select one student from each team to be "It".

Write on the chalkboard one word for each team from the provided rhyming word list. Make sure that each team knows its target word. Tell each student who is It to secretly write on his paper three words that rhyme with his team's word. Instruct each of the students who are not It to write one rhyming word. If teams do not have equal numbers of players, let one person who is not It from each of the "shorted" teams write two rhyming words. This will give each team equal scoring opportunities. The "double respondent" can be changed after each round, periodically, or not at all.

When all students are ready, have those who are It stand. Have the person who is standing from Team 1 ask a teammate what word he has written. The standing person must then tell if he himself has written that same answer. If so, the team earns a point. The next person from the same team then reveals his written answer. Again award a point for a match with the standing person, even if this player's answer is a match that has already been revealed. For example, if the person from Team 1 who is It has written "meat", "feet" and "sweet" to rhyme with the given word "eat", check all teammates' responses. If the first non-standing player has written "feet", the second "cheat", the third "sweet" and the fourth "feet", Team 1 earns three points because three players have written the same word (feet, feet, sweet) as the player who is It. Evaluate the correctness of each student's response, but award points for matches only. Repeat the procedure with Team 2, Team 3...

Begin round two by selecting a new person from each team to be It. Write another word for each team on the board, and play as described above. Continue the activity for as long as time allows, making sure that each person gets to be It at least once. When finished, total all scores. The team with the most points is the winner.

MODIFICATIONS: Provide a specified amount of time to write responses and allow <u>all</u> students to write as many words as they can think of to try to match the three (or more) responses written by the person who is It.

For lower grades or for students who have difficulty writing, have the person who is It whisper his answer to the teacher for recording. Then allow each classmate or teammate to write only the first letter or sound of his rhyming word.

Each person can keep his own score by being It for one round. When playing this way, each person can score up to three points, if at least one person in the class has written each of his words.

❄ ▭ ❖ ♒ ♌

Rhyming Word List

track	stool	straight
who	creep	here
what	plum	shock
bed	store	key
eat	float	sly
gray	crook	though
ace	croon	shut
wade	thrill	bland
stock	star	shale
steal	flake	flame
dream	stall	where

REAL STEAL

Students will provide two words that rhyme with a given word or set of words.

OBJECTIVES: Rhymes, Vocabulary
Strategies
Auditory association

TARGET POPULATION: Grades 1 & above
MATERIALS: Chalkboard and chalk
Rhyming Word List (provided)

PROCEDURE: Divide the class into Team "X" and Team "O". On the chalkboard draw a large 3 x 3 tic tac toe grid. Choose nine words from the provided list and write one in each of the nine boxes of the grid.

Have one person from Team X come to the board and choose the space where she would like to place her team's mark. Teammates may not help with this selection. She reads aloud the word in the selected square and then must name two words that rhyme with it. If both responses are correct, write her words in the same box as the original word, and then enter the team's mark (X) in an empty portion of the square. Play then passes to the other team.

The opposing team, remembering that the object of the game is to earn three of its marks in a row horizontally, vertically, or diagonally, still has the opportunity to select *any* of the nine boxes on the grid. The next player from this team may, if she wishes, try to win back a space already occupied by the opponent's mark. A player may do this by correctly providing two more words that rhyme with the words in the box. Write the newly revealed words inside the box as well. Then erase the opponent's X or O and replace it with the mark of the last correct respondent. Play again passes back to the original team.

If at any time neither or only one of the student's responses is correct, she receives no mark for her team and play passes to the opponent. Erase her one correct response, if any, from the square so that another student may use it later. Be certain that every team member has the opportunity to respond once before allowing anyone a second turn.

The first team to place three of its marks in a row wins the game.

If time allows, begin again. If there are only a few responses written in the squares from the first game, keep those words. If the grid contains many responses, erase them all and record new starting words in each box.

MODIFICATIONS: A 4 x 4 grid can be used to extend the game board. The team with four marks in a row or a mark in each corner is the winner.

Require each student to use the suggested rhyming words in sentences before awarding the square.

Allow teammates to assist with rhyming words.

Rhyming Word List

man	char	grow	fruit
shot	crash	jet	grace
gray	thing	that	grand
cheese	jail	shoe	skin
last	jam	chore	log
stun	grace	sweet	dig
rack	full	try	tall
where	flight	thrill	read
lad	bent	chest	bite
fed	slip	quit	great

LUCKY KENTUCKY

Students will guess a target word when given the category and a rhyming word.

OBJECTIVES: Classification
Rhymes
Vocabulary
Auditory association

TARGET POPULATION: Grades 1 - 5
MATERIALS: Rhyming Riddle List (provided)
Chalkboard & chalk
2 magnets or self-stick notes

PROCEDURE: Divide the class into two teams. On the chalkboard draw the following steps with as many levels as desired, and a flag at the top.

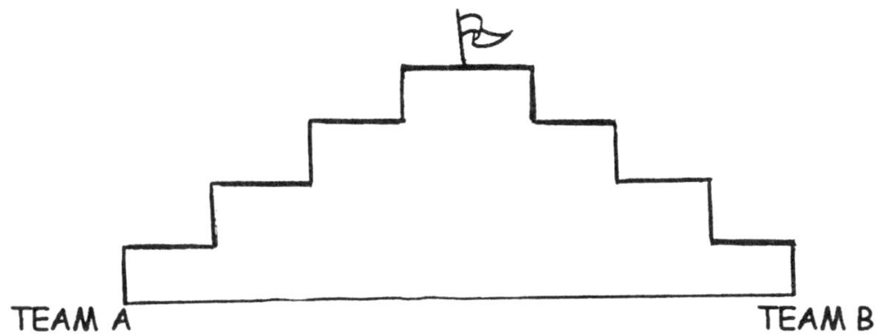

Use a magnet or self-stick note to represent each team, and place the markers on the bottom steps, one on each side. (It is also possible to use chalk to make X's that can be erased and replaced as the teams move up the steps.)

Inform students that they are to listen for the name of a category and then for a clue. The last word of the clue will rhyme with the intended answer. Read aloud one of the rhyming riddles to provide an example.

Have the first player from each team stand and prepare to respond. Read another rhyming riddle from the provided list. Either standing student may blurt out the answer as soon as she knows it. Each student is allowed only one response, however, and then whether correct or not, she must sit. If the first respondent's answer is incorrect, the other standing student may guess. If a student gives a correct response, move her team's marker one step closer to capturing the flag at the top.

If neither standing student is able to correctly identify the given riddle rhyme, ask for a volunteer from the class. In this case neither team advances toward the flag.

Have the second player from each team stand. Read the next riddle rhyme, and proceed as described above. Continue this procedure until everyone has had the opportunity to respond at least one time. Make sure that if students are given a second chance to respond, no one has the same opponent as in the first round. This will be done naturally if teams have an unequal number of players. If necessary, however, adjust one team so that different competitors are matched.

When a team reaches the top level and captures the flag, award that team one point. Move both markers back to the bottom levels and begin again. Continue for as long as time allows and then total all points. The team with the most points is the winner.

MODIFICATIONS: When one team captures the flag, move that team's marker to the bottom step but allow the opponent to continue from its current position.

❄ ⌘ ⚐ ❖ ♈ ♌ ● ⚐ ✌

Rhyming Riddle List

This STATE is LUCKY	Kentucky
In this TEXAS CITY there's a girl named ALICE	Dallas
This SPORT involves ROLLING	bowling
This young PET is not a GUPPY	puppy
Wear this CLOTHING to a DANCE	pants
This sharp UTENSIL is used by a WIFE	knife
This MUSICAL INSTRUMENT has a narrow MIDDLE	fiddle
This COLOR matches the sky and the water, TOO	blue
This BODY PART loves a ROSE	nose/toes
This STATE gets lots of RAIN	Maine
This CAR PART often stores JUNK	trunk
Shooting this BIRD is not LEGAL	eagle
This purple FRUIT has an oval SHAPE	grape
This kind of VEHICLE had better FLOAT	boat
In this BUILDING there might be a MOUSE	house
This kind of FURNITURE has to be STABLE	table
You won't want these INSECTS in your PANTS	ants
This kind of TREE is a favorite of MINE	pine
This BODY PART can sometimes do HARM	arm

This is the COLOR of a rainy DAY	gray
This MONTH often has a full MOON	June
This TIMEPIECE says tick-TOCK	clock
To play this SPORT, don't leave the ball in a LOCKER	soccer
This SERVING DISH is usually FLATTER	platter
This type of GEMSTONE can be worn by GIRLS	pearls
This kind of TREE is no JOKE	oak
This MONTH often has a sunny DAY	May
This is the DIRECTION that cowboys like BEST	west
This MUSICAL INSTRUMENT really sounds CUTE	flute
This VEGETABLE is often GREEN	bean
This VEHICLE is often driven by a family MAN	van
This BUG's body is often WIDER	spider
This may be the COLOR of a winter NIGHT	white
This ANIMAL sometimes takes more than his SHARE	bear/hare
In this kind of VEHICLE you travel with no FUSS	bus
This type of WEAPON is very NARROW	arrow
This brand of TRUCK is very HEAVY	Chevy
This FACIAL HAIR sometimes looks WEIRD	beard
This is a FEMALE whose name might be KATIE	lady
If you see this legless ANIMAL, be sure it's a FAKE	snake
This FAMILY MEMBER is like no OTHER	mother/brother
This is a PLACE to see animals, not just one or TWO	zoo
These YOUNG ANIMALS like looking for GRUBS	cubs
This stringed INSTRUMENT sounds really MELLOW	cello
This POWER TOOL can make a hole for you to FILL	drill
This FAMILY MEMBER is never a MISTER	sister
This BARNYARD ANIMAL is ridden, of COURSE	horse
This HAIR DECORATION may be tied, you KNOW	bow
If you dig up this CHEST, it may bring you PLEASURE	treasure
This kind of MAIL could make you feel BETTER	letter
This kind of DRINK is good for your DAUGHTER	water
This kind of CONTAINER might be filled with ROCKS	box
This MEAT SAUCE is served in the NAVY	gravy
This WRITING TOOL might be in your DEN	pen
This SHAPE might be seen in the sky AFAR	star

IN ORDER TO BE RIGHT

Students will produce sentences in which all words are arranged in alphabetical order.

OBJECTIVES: Vocabulary
Teamwork, Sentences
Creativity

TARGET POPULATION: Grades 2 & above
MATERIALS: Chalkboard & chalk
Paper & pencil/student

PROCEDURE: Divide the class into groups of three or four. All students should have paper and pencil, but designate only one student from each group to be the official recorder. On the left side of the chalkboard write the letter "A". Ask for volunteers to suggest 8 - 10 words that begin with "A", and record them on the board under that letter. Write the letter "B" a little to the right of the "A" list. Accept 8 - 10 "B" words and record them. Move right again and then do the same with "C" and "D" words.

Ask volunteers to try to make a short, logical sentence by combining in order one word from each letter's list. Responses might include, "All boys carry dogs", or "Andy brought chewy doughnuts." When students understand the task, instruct all teams to come up with their own sentences for the same four letters. They may use the words from the board or think of others, but they may use each word only once. After a short collaboration time, ask all recorders to write their sentences on the board. When all have finished, check the sentences for accuracy.

Start again by choosing four different consecutive letters, such as "L, M, N, O", or "S, T, U, V". Allow teams time to create their own sentences without brainstorming words with the class. Again have recorders write the sentences on the board. Suggest to students that it may be helpful to follow a sentence pattern, such as, "noun-verb-adjective-noun", or "adjective-noun-verb-adjective".

MODIFICATIONS: As a follow-up activity, have each student draw a picture to illustrate one of the sentences composed by her team.

Use a longer string of letters, or go through the entire alphabet making short sentences that tell a story in ABC order.

Have each student use her own initials to create three-word sentences. For example, Carrie Jane Harding might write: "Can James hop?" or "Cory just hurried."

Team points could be recorded on the chalkboard for each correct sentence.

In upper grades, have students take turns in order telling one line of a spontaneous conversation. The first word, and only the first word, of each line must begin with the next letter of the alphabet. Choose any letter to begin, and go from there. For example, a conversation may begin as follows:

"Fred just called me from the grocery store."
"Good, I've been waiting for him to phone."
"He needs a ride home."
"If you want, I'll go after him."
"Just wait a minute and we'll go together." etc.

Lovable Max Never Observed Plant Quotas.

FREQUENT PHRASES

Students will add a word to a given word to create a common phrase.

OBJECTIVES: Vocabulary, Strategies
Creativity
Auditory association

TARGET POPULATION: Grades 3 & above
MATERIALS: Phrase List (provided)
Pencil & paper/team

PROCEDURE: Divide the class into teams of 2 or 3 students. Give each team's designated recorder a piece of paper and a pencil. Tell students that points will be earned by any team that records a legitimate response *that no other team writes.* Each team will write only one response that must meet the following guidelines to be eligible for scoring:

1) The response must be a complete, single word.

2) The response must fit in the given blank as it is written in the phrase list. If, for example, the phrase says "___ day", the blank may not be moved to read "day ___".

3) The response must be frequently used with the given word in normal conversation. This combination could result in a compound word, a hyphenated word, or a frequently used phrase. The combination must be *commonly* used, as opposed to simply being *able* to be used. The response "normal day" or "nice day" might be considered to be an unacceptable response; whereas, "Mother's Day" or "snow day" would be acceptable. The teacher is the final judge as to word combinations that are deemed to be correct according to the rules of the game.

4) Synonyms reported by different teams are counted as different answers.

Select a phrase from the provided list and read it aloud. Give teams about 15 - 30 seconds to record one response that they think no other team will select. After time expires, begin checking answers for eligibility and nonduplication. Tally a point for each team that earns one.

If desired, assign a new recorder for each team for round two, and read another phrase from the provided list. Proceed as in round one, scoring points as they are earned.

Continue play for as long as time allows and then total all points. The team with the most points wins.

MODIFICATIONS: Have a designated player from each team secretly write a response to complete the phrase. Then have teammates try to *match* his phrase to earn points.

Phrase List (and examples)

HOME ___ (alone, town, grown)
___ DOOR (next, back, stage)
___ POLE (telephone, North, flag)
BIRD ___ (house, brain, bath)
___ BOARD (diving, sliding, card)
TEA ___ (bag, spoon, pot)
CHINESE ___ (checkers, proverb, restaurant)
GOLF ___ (cart, club, ball)
___ TABLE (picnic, kitchen, times)
APPLE ___ (sauce, pie, cider)
___ PAPER (wrapping, news, toilet)
___ TOWEL (beach, paper, bath)
SNOW ___ (suit, boots, man)
___ TAPE (video, masking, duct)
FIRE ___ (department, fly, truck)
BEACH ___ (ball, towel, blanket)
NATIONAL ___ (Geographic, park, anthem)
___ MILK (skim, chocolate, butter)
___ CHAIR (rocking, high, electric)
WATER ___ (bed, wings, filter)
ICE ___ (cube, skates, cream)
___ ROAD (paved, dirt, Rocky)
___ DOG (bull, top, hot)
___ SCHOOL (private, elementary, finishing)
WEATHER ___ (vane, man, map)
LEFT ___ (over, field, out)
ONE ___ (third, way, another)
LONG ___ (underwear, gone, shot)
GREEN ___ (bean, house, light)

WEDDING ___ (bells, gift, cake)
___ BEAN (lima, jelly, soy)
___ BAG (tea, grab, shopping)
___ BALL (base, crystal, foot)
GET ___ (up, lost, serious)
___ ROLL (egg, pay, honor)
GO ___ (fish, away, crazy)
___ UP (stand, close, pick)
UNDER ___ (pressure, water, stand)
___ LIGHT (night, star, flash)
___ HORSE (Charlie, rocking, hobby)
___ PAN (dish, Peter, cake)
TURN ___ (around, table, off)
___ FOOD (fast, dog, Mexican)
___ PIT (arm, bar-b-que, peach)
___ SALAD (potato, chicken, egg)
TOP ___ (hat, dog, ten)
___ HEAD (red, block, air)
CHECK ___ (up, book, out)
SHOE ___ (horn, box, store)
___ CAKE (birthday, chocolate, pan)
___ STORM (thunder, brain, snow)
EASTER ___ (Bunny, basket, Sunday)
___ CARD (credit, birthday, phone)
___ DRUM (ear, bass, bongo)
___ ROOM (dining, living, mush)
___ BLANKET (beach, electric, security)
___ WELL (wishing, get, oh)
TV ___ (dinner, set, Guide)

MEANINGFUL CHANGES

Students will change one word in a given sentence to make a meaningful new sentence.

OBJECTIVES: Vocabulary
Sentences
Creativity

TARGET POPULATION: Grades 2 - 6
MATERIALS: Chalkboard & chalk
Sentence Starter List (provided)

PROCEDURE: Divide the class into two teams and have them face each other in two lines, as in a traditional spelling bee. Write a sentence from the provided list on the chalkboard. Read it aloud to ensure that all students know the sentence. The object of the activity is to have each player in turn change one, and only one, word to make a meaningful new sentence.

The first person from Team 1 will respond first. She will state her new sentence, substituting *one* change for a word on the board. If she is correct, cross the original word from the sentence and write the replacement word beneath it. The student remains standing. If she is incorrect, however, she must return to her seat.

In either case play passes to the first person from Team 2. This player must now change a *different* word to make another *meaningful* sentence. Each new sentence must include all previous changes. Again write the new word on the board under the word that it replaced. Once a word from the original sentence has been changed, allow no more changes to that word.

The following is an example of how a sentence may be modified:

Original sentence: ~~The~~ horse jumped quickly over the white fence.
HER ~~horse~~ jumped quickly over the white fence.
Her DOG jumped ~~quickly~~ over the white fence.
Her dog jumped LAZILY over the white ~~fence.~~
Her dog ~~jumped~~ lazily over the white CHAIR.
Her dog CLIMBED lazily ~~over~~ the white chair.
Her dog climbed lazily UNDER the white chair. etc.

The sentence on the board, however, will look like this:

~~The horse jumped quickly over the white fence~~.
Her dog climbed lazily under a wooden chair.

Play passes back and forth between teams as each person in turn tries to follow the rules to produce a meaningful new sentence. A player must be seated if she is unable to do so when there is still at least one change to be made. Play continues with the same sentence starter form the provided list until two people in a row, one from each team, are unable to make a meaningful change in the sentence, or until all words have been replaced. Suggest possible changes to words that remain. Choose a new sentence starter and write it on the board. Play continues with team members who are still standing. No one may suggest a replacement word that was used in any previous sentence.

The game is over when time runs out, or when only one player remains standing.

MODIFICATIONS: ⚐ ❄ ❖ ✋ ⚐ ⌘ ● ♌

Sentence Starter List

The shiny car raced quickly around the track.
My friend, Mona, put some clothes into the boxes.
Her aunt can speak Russian well.
Elephants and clowns paraded past my house.
Loud country music was playing on the radio.
Rabbits ran everywhere in our yard.
In Millersville three men were arrested yesterday.
Six boys climbed the old apple tree last Saturday.
Every winter my family goes skiing.
Several people sang solos during the recital.
My grandfather caught a really huge fish last night.
My lazy dog was sleeping under our porch.
The horse jumped quickly over the white fence.

THE RIGHT RELATIONSHIP

Students will tell how if the meaning of one given word is the same as, a kind of, or a part of another given word.

OBJECTIVES: Vocabulary, Thinking
Synonyms, Relationships
Auditory association

TARGET POPULATION: Grades 3 & above
MATERIALS: Chalkboard & chalk
Sentence List (provided)
[1], [2] & [3] cards (copy 1 set/student from appendix)

PROCEDURE: Give each student a [1] card, a [2] card, and a [3] card. On the chalkboard write the following answer key for the number cards:

[1] = a kind of [2] = a part of [3] = the same as

Instruct students that holding up a [1] card indicates that they have chosen "a kind of" as an answer, [2] means "a part of", etc. Make sure that all students understand this correspondence by asking them to hold up the card that means "the same as"... When students understand begin the game.

Read to the class a sentence from the provided list. Instruct students that they are to determine which phrase from the chalkboard correctly completes the given sentence. For example, if the sentence is "Chocolate is ______ pudding", students who understand the instructions and the concepts will prepare to hold up their [1] cards ("a kind of"). Each student conceals against his chest the card that reflects his answer. He also turns the unused number cards face down on his desk.

When all students are ready say, "Raise your cards", and all students do so simultaneously. No student is permitted to change his selection at this point. Explain correct answers to any student who is having difficulty.

Continue the activity with additional sentences from the provided list.

MODIFICATIONS: This activity can be played as a game if the class is divided into teams. Team points can be earned by individual members responding correctly or by the spokesperson of the group who correctly reports its consensus. If individual players are scoring points for their teams, be certain that all teams have an equal number of players, or announce that "extra" players actually earn points for all teams. Extra players could also be used as judges who announce correct answers after seeing all responses.

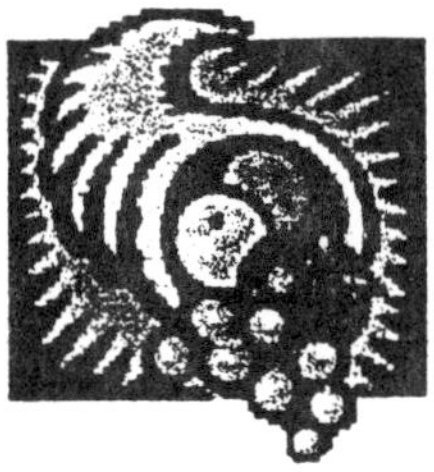

Sentence List

1 = a kind of   2 = a part of   3 = the same as

A finger is __2__ a hand.
Chocolate is __1__ a pudding.
The frosting is __2__ a cake.
A wall is __2__ a house.
A bucket is __3__ a pail.
An eraser is __2__ a pencil.
A book is __2__ a library.
A tail is __2__ a dog.
A seesaw is __3__ a teeter-totter.
A handle is __2__ a lunchbox.
Rock & roll is __1__ music.
Glue is __2__ a postage stamp.
A TV is __3__ a television.
A principal is __2__ a school.
A refrigerator is __1__ appliance.
A lyric is __2__ a song.
A sofa is __3__ a couch.
A rose is __1__ a plant.
A girl is __1__ female.
The monitor is __2__ a computer.
Arithmetic is __3__ math.
Ham is __1__ meat.
Stripes are __2__ the US's flag.
A nickel is __1__ coin.
Claws are __2__ a lion.
The chorus is __2__ a song.
A cobra is __1__ a snake.
A feline is __3__ a cat.
The ace is __2__ a deck of cards.
USA is __3__ America.
Jealousy is __1__ feeling.
A motorcycle is __1__ vehicle.

A mom is __3__ a mother.
Water is __1__ a liquid.
Maple is __1__ a tree
A chicken is __3__ a hen.
A leg is __2__ a chair.
A convertible is __1__ a car.
A banana is __1__ a fruit.
A cardinal is __1__ a bird.
Garbage is __3__ trash.
A child is __2__ class.
A stomach is __3__ belly.
Carpet is __1__ floor covering
A French fry is __1__ a potato.
A tree is __2__ a forest.
A piece is __3__ part.
A car is __3__ an automobile.
A birthday is __1__ celebration.
A human being is __3__ a person.
A couple is __3__ a pair.
A basement is __2__ a house.
A stem is __2__ a fruit.
A tiger is __1__ a cat.
The volume control is __2__ a TV.
A poodle is a __1__ dog.
Unhealthy is __3__ sick.
A sister is __2__ a family.
The gymnasium is __2__ a school.
The bleachers are __2__ a stadium.
An airplane is __1__ transportation.
An ocean is __3__ a sea.
Cattle are __3__ cows.
A lady is __3__ a woman.

WHAT DO YOU MEAN?

Students will decide whether the information in a given sentence is redundant, contradictory, or logical.

OBJECTIVES: Vocabulary
Auditory association & memory

TARGET POPULATION: Grades 3 & above
MATERIALS: Sentence list (provided)
Chalkboard & chalk
[1], [2] & [3] cards (copy 1 set/team from appendix)

PROCEDURE: Write the following on the chalkboard and discuss what each means:

1. redundant (needless repetition)
2. contradictory (opposite of something else said)
3. logical (making sense)

Divide students into 3 - 4 teams. Give the first player from each team a set of number cards ([1], [2], [3]) and have him stand. Only those players holding number cards may respond. Each card holder will be holding up the number card that indicates his choice for a response. A [1] card indicates that "redundant" is the chosen response, [2] means "contradictory", and [3] means "logical".

Read a sentence from the provided list. Each standing student with number cards should select the number that indicates his response and hold the card against his chest. Unused number cards should be turned face down so that others cannot see them. When everyone is ready, have all reveal their cards simultaneously.

Award one point to each team whose player has responded correctly. If the given sentence was not logical, ask any class member to explain the problem.

Then have each card holder pass his number cards to the next player on his team. Repeat the above procedure, awarding points as they are earned.

Continue by passing cards to new respondents and reading new sentences for as long as time allows. Total all points when finished. The team with the most points is the winner.

MODIFICATIONS: ❖ ● ♒ ⚐ ✎ ♌ ❄ ⌘ ⚑

Sentence List

(R = Redundant L = Logical C = Contradictory)

R) She was blind and couldn't see anything.
C) His clean-shaven face had a magnificent beard.
L) Irene introduced me to her mother's uncle.
R) I thought that he was being redundant over and over.
C) Robert wore a solid-colored shirt with blue stripes.
R) The naked boy had no clothes on.
C) The ailing bird silently squawked all through the night.
R) We sent the paperwork to the office of the secretary's office.
R) The fragrant flowers had a smell about them.
C) The totally bald man couldn't get his hair to look right.
L) The three horses ran swiftly across the meadow.
R) That girl by the fence is a female.
R) My best friend joined the army in the military.
L) Dad loves to watch hockey games on TV.
R) Her reddish curly hair wasn't straight.
C) The smooth, soft, silken scarf felt really rough to my face.
L) If you turn left, you will be headed in the right direction.
C) We listened to the opera on the country music station.
C) Her hair blew wildly in the breezeless night air.
C) The newborn toddler drank his milk quickly.
R) The identical twins look exactly the same.
C) I sent my name and address along with my anonymous donation.
L) She served the food as quickly as she could.
C) Barbie's blue denim skirt clashed with her matching blue denim blouse.
L) The principal made an announcement about the meeting that afternoon.
R) The veterinarian worked with animals.
C) The teacher contradicted me because she agreed with what I said.
C) The pot of boiling water burned me as I removed it from the freezer.
C) The decision to have a party was unanimous, but two kids voted against it.
R) I think we should repaint your room over.
L) All prisoners are allowed to watch TV on Saturday night.
C) The vegetarians enjoyed a meal of steak and potatoes.
C) The dead man was barely alive.
C) He strained his back muscles as he lifted the lightweight boxes.
C) He accidentally wrecked his car on purpose.

WHAT GIVES?

Students will show that they know the meaning of given verbs by their responses to given questions.

OBJECTIVES: Vocabulary
Auditory association
Creativity

TARGET POPULATION: Grades 2 & above
MATERIALS: Action Question List (provided)
Chalkboard & chalk

PROCEDURE: Have all students stand and form a large circle around the classroom. Announce that every other student, or every student wearing blues jeans (or brown shoes or glasses...), must sit down in her place on the circle. About one-half of the class should be standing and the other half sitting. Only standing students will respond during the first round. Choose any standing student to begin. Ask her one of the "What?" questions from the provided list. If her response is appropriate, she remains standing. Anytime a response is inappropriate, the student must sit in her place in the circle. Ask for clarification, if necessary.

Have the next standing student respond to the same question. Continue asking that question around the circle until two correct responses are received. When the entire standing group has had the opportunity to respond one time, tell all standing students to sit and all sitting students to stand. Select a new standing student to begin this round. Continue with the same question if two correct answers have not yet been revealed, or select a new question from the provided list. Continue playing additional rounds by switching sitting and standing students, and asking additional questions.

Each time a student is incorrect with his response, write the verb in question on the board so that a review can be done at the end of the activity.

Continue playing as long as time allows. It may be necessary to occasionally adjust the number of standing and sitting students so that neither group is depleted. Playing in this fashion gives students who are having difficulty up to twice the number of opportunities to respond.

MODIFICATIONS: Place students in teams and have them brainstorm as many answers as they can in a given amount of time. Award points, if desired, based on the number of appropriate, unduplicated responses.

Action Question List

What quenches?
What bounces?
What drips?
What smells?
What rips?
What swings?
What burns?
What freezes?
What rolls?
What slams?
What blooms?
What soars?
What burrows?
What hangs?
What waddles?
What hibernates?
What bucks?
What hops?
What burns?
What stings?
What prances?
What squirms?
What concludes?
What rotates?
What topples?
What wiggles?
What collapses?
What increases?
What escapes?
What glows?

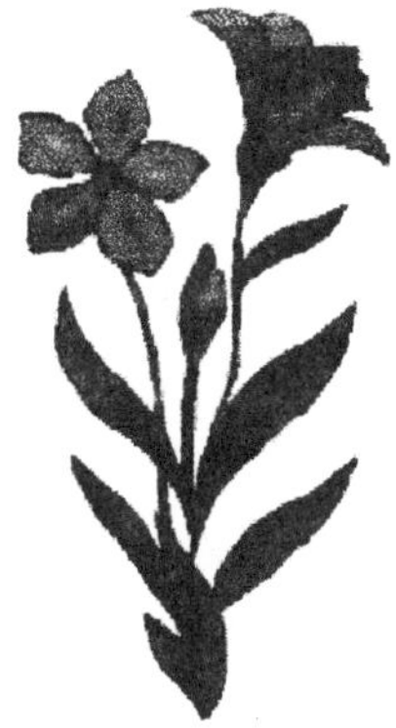

What frays?
What slithers?
What disintegrates?
What warps?
What crumbles?
What increases?
What melts?
What pivots?
What signals?
What swims?
What joins?
What flattens?
What wrinkles?
What explodes?
What sinks?
What decays?
What groans?
What turns?
What reverses?
What cracks?
What clangs?
What irritates?
What flutters?

What delays?
What tarnishes?
What varies?
What whistles?
What continues?
What evolves?
What bends?
What flows?
What snaps?
What frightens?
What floats?
What itches?
What accelerates?
What erupts?
What stains?
What shrieks?
What drills?
What aches?
What drains?
What shatters?
What revolves?
What dribbles?
What paces?
What vibrates?
What quakes?
What flies?
What rubs?
What curls?
What dangles?
What smokes?

WHERE IN THE WORLD?

Teams will provide three words or phrases that meaningfully complete a carrier sentence.

OBJECTIVES: Vocabulary
Auditory association
Context clues

TARGET POPULATION: Grades 1-3
MATERIALS: Paper & pencil/team
Chalkboard & chalk
Sentence List (provided)

PROCEDURE: Divide the class into teams of 4 or 5 students and give paper and pencil to each team's designated recorder. Students will be attempting to complete a given sentence with one or more answers. Responses should be creative since answers duplicated by other teams will earn no points.

Read aloud one of the sentences from the provided list. Allow teams a short time to write three words or phrases that will appropriately and meaningfully complete that sentence. Remind students to be sure to pay attention to the preposition that precedes the blank. Their answers must appropriately complete the prepositional phrase. For example, if the chosen carrier sentence is "She slept on _____", the answer "my sofa" would be correct but "my room" would not.

After the time limit expires, all recorders go to the chalkboard and simultaneously write their three answers. No recorder should watch what the others are writing. When finished recorders return to their seats.

Read aloud the sentence with the first answer listed on the board. If the class agrees that it is a good response, check the lists written by the other teams. If the same response appears on any other team's list, cross it off each list and award no points for that answer. If the answer is legitimate and appears on no other team's list, score one point for the team that recorded it on the board.

Check all other written responses for that sentence and record all points. Each team could earn up to three points per round by writing responses duplicated by no other team. Once a recorder writes a response on the board, it may not be written by any team for the rest of the activity.

Continue with additional rounds by choosing new recorders and sentences. Follow the procedure as explained above. Play continues for as long as time allows. Total all points and declare the team with the most to be the winner.

MODIFICATIONS: Do not allow responses to be proper nouns such as "New York" or "Burger King". This will encourage more creative thinking.

For younger students or those who cannot write, record 5 whispered answers from the responding team. Then allow each player from the other teams to guess these responses. The guessing team gets a point if a player's verbal response matches one of the answers on the whispered list. For each answer that is <u>not</u> guessed, award one point to the team that created the list.

Sentence List

I got my hair cut at _____.
I ate pizza in _____.
Mary slept on _____.
Dean fell off of_____.
The bear tripped over the _____.
Mom and I shopped in _____.
Our family vacationed at _____.
We pitched a tent near _____.
The pilot flew us to _____.
Write your name on the _____.
Put that box beside the _____.
The old man shuffled around _____.
The spider crawled under _____.
The truck drove through _____.
The vase fell off the _____.
Sam took a cup from _____.
The fish swam all around _____.
We collected seashells in _____.
Jim read his books at _____.
Wrap this around _____.
Hide your money under the _____.
Muffin climbed into the _____.

APPENDIX

ANTONYM RESOURCE LIST

simple - complex	unusual - common	major - minor	spend - save
omit - include	past - future	dirty - clean	positive - negative
increase - decrease	ignite - extinguish	asleep - awake	excited - calm
harmful - helpful	front - back	always - never	same - different
busy - idle	absent - present	raw - cooked	best - worst
permit - forbid	forward - backward	pass - fail	accept - refuse
compare - contrast	fact - fiction	public - private	length - width
innocent - guilty	crooked - straight	raw - cooked	deep - shallow
victory - defeat	spicy - bland	give - take	fragile - sturdy
remember - forget	generous - stingy	floor - ceiling	near - far
worthless - priceless	mountain - valley	empty - full	good - evil
stale - fresh	wise - stupid	friend - enemy	plain - fancy
interior - exterior	clear - vague	polite - rude	arrive - depart
permanent - temporary	whole - part	birth - death	giant - miniature
those - these	smooth - rough	dusk - dawn	beginning - end
weak - strong	offense - defense	seldom - often	wild - tame
inferior - superior	separate - together	sorrow - joy	comedy - trajedy
tight - loose	maximum - minimum	brave - cowardly	question - answer

---

SYNONYM RESOURCE LIST

summit - peak	spicy - hot	pillow - cushion	hurt - harm
dirt - soil	reject - refuse	unusual - rare	foe - enemy
gigantic - enormous	require - need	totally - entirely	vacant - empty
option - choice	damp - moist	peaceful - tranquil	timid - shy
vanish - disappear	fix - mend	teach - instruct	desire - want
fantastic - wonderful	glasses - spectacles	foolish - silly	tardy - late
ask - request	answer - respond	copy - imitate	near - close
brave - courageous	sorrow - grief	odd - peculiar	beg - plead
assist - help	more - additional	fear - fright	real - genuine
smell - odor	often - frequently	ache - pain	shut - close
under - below	hatchet - ax	teacher - instructor	allow - permit
beg - plead	identical - exact	friend - comrade	final - last
fragile - breakable	leave - depart	wealthy - rich	truth - fact
intelligent - smart	maybe - perhaps	search - seek	dead - deceased
scenery - landscape	student - pupil	view - watch	change - modify
injure - hurt	correct - right	surpass - excel	find - discover
create - make	funny - humorous	tale - story	merit - worth
limit - boundary	also - additionally	mistake - error	current - flow

CATEGORY RESOURCE LIST

EASIER

white foods
animal babies
things that shut
things found in trees
things in an airplane
lunchbox foods
musical instruments
camping gear
winter clothing
2-syllable words
things with wheels
2-letter words
things that scare kids
famous places
things that float
things in a bedroom
things that can hurt you
cowboy needs
breakfast foods
things at the beach
pizza toppings
things in a girl's purse
parts of a taco
table-setting things
transportation
things to put on bread
famous singers/bands
things that have lights
electrical things
words that tell size
ways to use water
kinds of mall stores
school subjects
parts of a face
words starting with "m"
words spelled with "oo"
reasons to get punished
things that are not flat
things that fit in pockets
things needing batteries

sports
birds
dogs
machines
flowers
candy
shapes
red things
meats
computer games
superheroes
holidays
jewelry
drinks
insects
tools
countries
liquids
vegetables
relatives
"kiddie" songs
sour things
kid clubs
feelings
cereals
bathroom needs
square things
zoo animals
water toys
math words
car parts
kinds of cats
buildings
trees
traffic signs
furniture
smelly things
park things
entertainers
cold things

MORE DIFFICULT

types of dances
winter Olympic events
magic tricks
things with holes
famous detectives
monsters/creatures
international money
orchestra instruments
hyphenated words
U. S. presidents
famous women
childhood illnesses
herbs/spices
items sold in pairs
circus performers
dairy products
fairy tales
things that go around
toothpaste brands
4-syllable words
game shows
kinds of parties
stringed instruments
newspaper cartoons
black & white things
brands of soap
kinds of cheese
things made of metal
things that give off heat
news/sportscasters
kinds of chairs
female movie stars
natural disasters
suffixes
Indian tribes
means of communication
things with flashing lights
things that need painting
bodies of water
synonyms for "street"

authors
containers
footwear
wars
famous pairs
palindromes
kinds of fish
planets
abbreviations
"qu" words
military ranks
religions
fasteners
compound words
hospital workers
cereal brands
Dr. Seuss books
precipitation
computer terms
prefixes
striped things
things that melt
kinds of boats
TV networks
bad habits
rivers
sports violations
prepositions
islands
conjunctions
things that ring
famous doctors
internal organs
pointy things
inventors
things with seats
gemstones
fragile things
condiments
islands

COMPOUND WORD RESOURCE LIST

windsock	playmate	chatterbox	bloodshot
easygoing	hairdresser	marketplace	nutcracker
padlock	breakthrough	offspring	killjoy
penthouse	outsmart	cheapskate	jackknife
wedlock	turnpike	secondhand	nightclub
wallflower	sharpshooter	countdown	playpen
blabbermouth	gentlemen	elsewhere	hearsay
layoff	lockjaw	meatball	boxcar
backhand	nosebleed	catwalk	downpour
icebox	moonbeam	parkway	sinkhole
wasteland	grapevine	ashtray	barnyard
elkhound	ferryboat	safekeeping	manhunt
offhand	gangplank	keepsake	landlord
racetrack	lumberjack	passageway	vineyard
birdbrain	gingerbread	openminded	whiplash
timepiece	chainsmoke	battlefield	dreadlocks
handcuff	mainland	newsworthy	newcomer
brainwash	peacemaker	bathhouse	headstone
nobleman	tenderfoot	oncoming	fishbowl
bedpost	dashboard	doorknob	knucklehead
levelheaded	lightweight	eyedropper	matchbook
figurehead	baseboard	deadeye	earsplitting
flatbed	hardheaded	screenplay	background
lawmaker	candlestick	handlebar	upset
tattletale	skyjack	roughhouse	flowerpot
jaywalk	nameplate	sawmill	earthshaking
drawbridge	lamebrain	meanwhile	stingray
firsthand	piggyback	backdrop	mastermind
ourselves	railroad	windowshop	foolhardy
greenhouse	shortsighted	eavesdrop	peephole
bagpipe	caretaker	linebacker	sightseeing
warlock	bellhop	laughingstock	patchwork
bottleneck	ripcord	doomsday	worthwhile
seaboard	potluck	lifesaver	oftentimes
filmstrip	stairwell	handwriting	cowhand
roommate	elbowroom	otherwise	printout
blackbird	whoever	brainstorm	scarecrow
eyewitness	fainthearted	eyesore	jigsaw
latticework	rainwater	schoolmaster	slingshot
skywriting	timberline	thumbtack	watchdog
homestretch	driftwood	motherland	backtrack

CONTRACTION RESOURCE LIST

I'd	I'll	I've	I'm	wouldn't
you'd	you'll	you've	you're	shouldn't
he'd	he'll	he's	it's	couldn't
she'd	she'll	she's	that's	who's
we'd	we'll	we've	we're	what's
they'd	they'll	they've	they're	there's
isn't	aren't	wasn't	weren't	where's
haven't	hasn't	hadn't	can't	how's
don't	doesn't	didn't	won't	Gabe's...

Colloquial Contractions

what'll	who'll	where'll	that'll	it'll
what'd	who'd	where'd	how'd	it'd
what're	who're	when's	how're	where've
what've	should've	would've	could've	how've

HETERONYM RESOURCE LIST

convert: con'-vert / con-vert'
subject: sub'-ject / sub-ject'
project: pro-ject' / pro'-ject
contrast: con'-trast / con-trast'
resume: re-sume' / res'-u-me
console: con'-sole / con-sole'
digest: di-gest' / di'-gest
polish: pol'-ish / Po'-lish
compress: com-press' / com'-press
intimate: in'-ti-mate / in'-tim-ate'
suspect: sus'-pect / su-spect'
convict: con'-vict / con-vict'
produce: pro'-duce / pro-duce'
alternate: al'-ter-nit / al'-ter-nate
read: red / reed
live: liv / liev
dove: duv / doev
tear: teer / tare
lead: led / leed
bass: base / bass
sow: soe / sow
reside: re-zide' / re-side'
reject: re-ject' / re'-ject
separate: sep'-a-rate / sep'-rit

minute: min'-ute / mi-nute'
perfect: per'-fect / per-fect'
invalid: in'-va-lid / in-val'-id
invite: in-vite' / in'-vite
contest: con'-test / con-test'
refuse: re-fuse' / ref'-use
content: con'-tent / con-tent'
record: re-cord' / rec'-ord
present: pre-sent' / pres'-ent
object: ob'-ject / ob-ject'
proceeds: pro-ceeds' / pro'ceeds
desert: des'-ert / de-sert'
permit: per'-mit / per-mit'
progress: prog'-ress / pro-gress'
bow: bow / boe
wound: wownd / woond
wind: winned / wined
number: num'-ber / num'-er
does: duz / doze
close: cloze / close
resort: re-zort' / re-sort'
resign: re-zine' / re-sine'
reserve: re-zerve' / re-serve'
conduct: con'-duct / con-duct'

HOMOPHONE RESOURCE LIST

bear - bare
blue - blew
red - read
flower - flour
right - write - rite
hall - haul
here - hear
waist - waste
doe - dough
thrown - throne
deer - dear
seize - sees - seas
so - sow - sew
steak - stake
colonel - kernel
allowed - aloud
aisle - isle - I'll
billed - build
guessed - guest
main - mane
cellar - seller
chews - choose
oar - or - ore
paced - paste
peak - peek
root - route
flea - flee
medal - metal - meddle
base - bass
ewe - you - yew
altar - alter
pray - prey
pride - pried
ring - wring
lesson - lessen
peer - pier
stationary - stationery
moose - mousse
martial - marshal
whose - who's
days - daze

beet - beat
wood - would
rain - reign - rein
four - for
road - rode - rowed
scent - sent - cent
sealing - ceiling
peace - piece
pair - pear - pare
pail - pale
bored - board
site - sight - cite
son - sun
him - hymn
creak - creek
hoarse - horse
die - dye
forth - fourth
hair - hare
made - maid
been - bin
ducked - duct
none - nun
pain - pane
pedal - peddle - petal
raise - rays
chute - shoot
dew - do - due
close - clothes
fined - find
band - banned
gorilla - guerilla
maize - maze
some - sum
idle - idol
rose - rows
suite - sweet
profit - prophet
plum - plumb
there - their
hose - hoes

heel - heal - he'll
weak - week
flu - flew
grate - great
sail - sale
sea - see
way - weigh
fare - fair
toe - tow
nose - knows
in - inn
knew - gnu - new
buy - by - bye
acts - ax
desert - dessert
hole - whole
feat - feet
groan - grown
heard - herd
cereal - serial
loan - lone
won - one
overdo - overdue
pause - paws
sole - soul
prince - prints
core - corps
boar - bore
karat - carrot
air - err - heir
halve - have
frays - phrase
manor - manner
steal - steel
oh - owe
real - reel
naval - navel
pore - pour -poor
pole - poll
its - it's
mind - mined

MULTIMEANING WORD RESOURCE LIST (HOMOGRAPHS)

skip
ball
hide
mine
pitcher
yard
bill
pick
bit
play
soil
stranger
bow
felt
buck
pop
can
punch
rest
left
check
cool
peep
line
draw
duck
round
trail
box
spring
flounder
sink
cold
stand
break
bug
fiddle
fence
late
lodge

press
bark
ice
iron
set
watch
jar
pipe
block
point
shine
shoot
kid
pen
last
pound
change
race
right
charge
lie
mind
bowl
second
corn
face
screen
dart
counter
squash
blue
set
toast
turn
hard
branch
organ
smoke
kind
cable

tune
ground
bank
jam
over
train
drill
game
joker
tick
loaf
color
cross
pass
clip
tag
leaves
surface
paddle
letter
patch
date
might
down
faint
bulb
seal
appendix
show
major
free
tie
plot
safe
page
calf
brave
lot
hot
dice

felt
hang
hail
bat
plane
top
fly
trunk
key
deal
match
switch
break
step
rock
swallow
saw
place
club
part
rose
mean
miss
fall
nail
mold
file
frame
company
order
track
snap
building
strip
cross
present
post
spoke
rich
plant

ruler
head
hand
bed
run
season
fine
grade
ruler
bear
tackle
feet
bright
frost
roll
story
lap
crane
range
type
chest
light
deck
park
brush
note
shape
blind
spray
drop
star
shade
trace
class
row
ring
pass
fair
even
shed

PREFIX RESOURCE LIST

anti-	antifreeze, antiperspirant
auto-	autobiography, autopilot
bi-	biannually, bicycle
co-	cooperate, codirectors
de-	defrost, deactivate
dis-	disagree, disintegrate
ex-	ex-wife, ex-convict
fore-	forethought, forehead
hyper-	hyperactive, hypertension
il-	illogical, illegal
im-	improper, impossible
in-	insufficient, inhuman
inter-	intertwine, international
intra-	intravenous, intramurals
mal-	malnourished, malfunction
micro-	microwave, microscope
mid-	midnight, midway
mis-	misspell, misunderstand
mono-	monochromatic, monotone
multi-	multicolored, multitalented
non-	nonstop, nonviolent
out-	outline, outside
	outgrew, outmaneuvered
over-	overeat, overthrow
	overhead, overhang
post-	postdate, postgame
pre-	preheat, preview
re-	replay, rewrite
semi-	semicircle, semiretired
sub-	subway, submarine
super-	supersonic, superhuman
trans-	transplant, transcontinental
tri-	triangle, tripod
ultra-	ultralight, ultraviolet
un-	unreliable, unforgettable
uni-	unicycle, uniform

SUFFIX RESOURCE LIST

-able	managable, reliable
-al	musical, historical
-ance	appearance, defiance
-ant	defendant, assistant
-ation	combination, sensation
-dom	kingdom, freedom
-ee	employee, trainee
-eer	profiteer, mountaineer
-ence	preference, difference
-ent	respondent, president
-er	rescuer, reporter
	smaller, noisier
-ess	actress, lioness
-est	freshest, closest
-ful	forgetful, playful
-hood	neighborhood, childhood
-ian	musician, electrician
-ic	angelic, alcoholic
-ion	election, reaction
-ish	yellowish, devilish
-ism	heroism, criticism
-ist	flutist, manicurist
-itis	laryngitis, sinusitis
-ity	nationality, reality
-ive	detective, attractive
-less	senseless, motionless
-like	childlike, manlike
-ly	uniquely, rapidly
-ment	argument, apartment
-ness	gentleness, business
-or	actor, elevator
-ous	glamourous, ridiculous
-s	sparrows, mustaches
-ship	courtship, hardship
-some	lonesome, awesome
-tion	intervention, convention
-ward	westward, downward
-y	grumpy, icy

1	2	3
4	5	6

TICKETS

TICKET	TICKET	TICKET
TICKET	TICKET	TICKET
TICKET	TICKET	TICKET

DOT-TO-DOT GRID

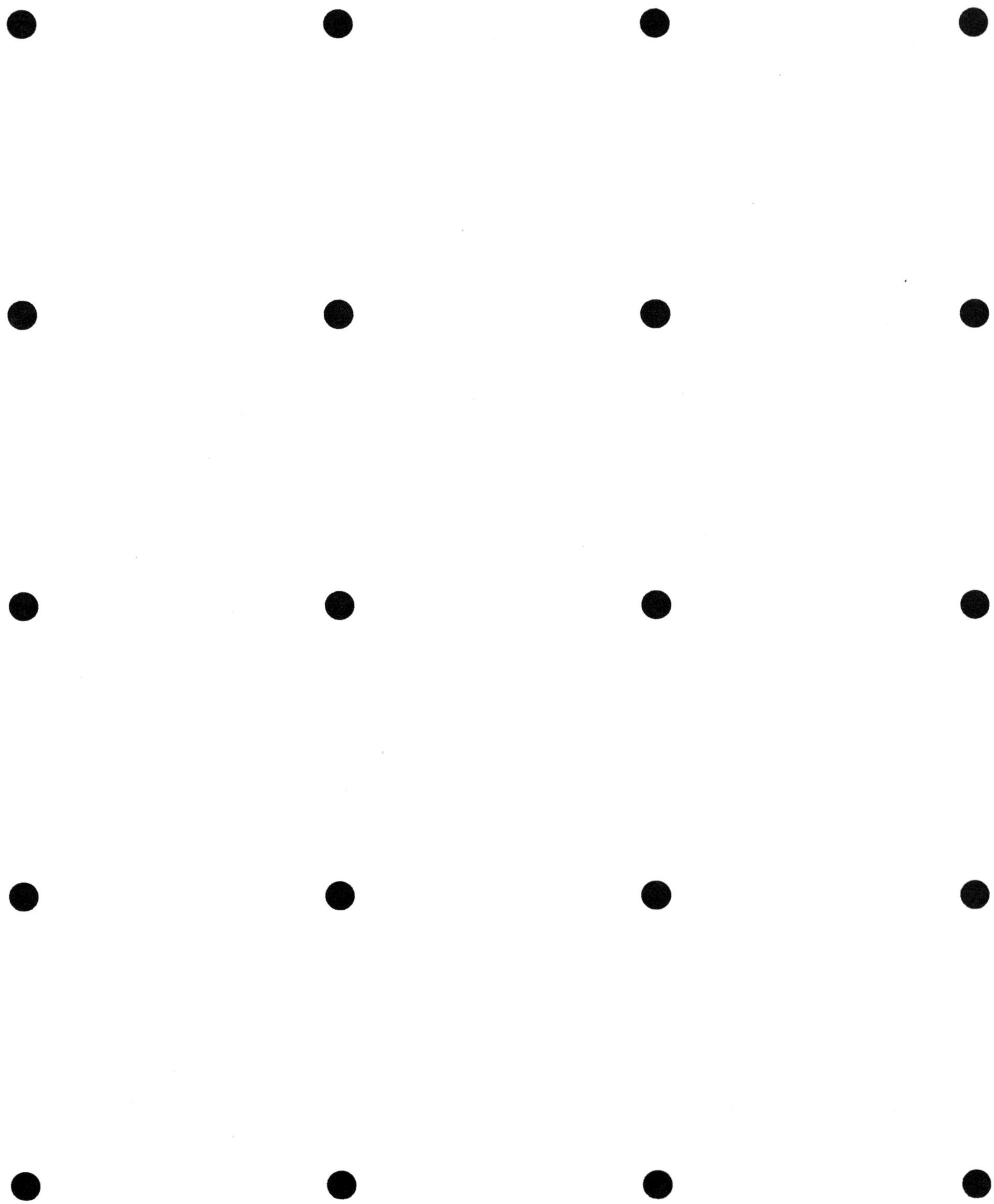